Adalena Kavanagh

ELISA GABBERT

Any Person Is the Only Self

Elisa Gabbert is the author of *Normal Distance*, *The Unreal-ity of Memory*, and several other collections of poetry, essays, and criticism. She writes the On Poetry column for *The New York Times*, and her work has appeared in *Harper's Magazine*, *The Atlantic*, *The Believer*, *The New York Times Magazine*, *The New York Review of Books*, and other publications.

Any Person Is the Only Self

Any Person Is the Only Self

Essays

Elisa Gabbert

FSG Originals

FARRAR, STRAUS AND GIROUX

NEW YORK

FSG Originals
Farrar, Straus and Giroux
120 Broadway, New York 10271

Library of Congress Cataloging-in-Publication Data
Names: Gabbert, Elisa, author.
Title: Any person is the only self : essays / Elisa Gabbert.
Description: First edition. | New York : FSG Originals /
 Farrar, Straus and Giroux, 2024. | Includes bibliographical
 references.
Identifiers: LCCN 2023051859 | ISBN 9780374605896
 (paperback)
Subjects: LCGFT: Essays.
Classification: LCC PS3607.A227 A65 2020 | DDC 814/.6—
 dc23/eng/20231226
LC record available at https://lccn.loc.gov/2023051859

Our books may be purchased in bulk for promotional, educational,
or business use. Please contact your local bookseller or
the Macmillan Corporate and Premium Sales Department at
1-800-221-7945, extension 5442, or by email at
MacmillanSpecialMarkets@macmillan.com.

www.fsgoriginals.com • www.fsgbooks.com
Follow us on social media at @fsgoriginals and @fsgbooks

1 3 5 7 9 10 8 6 4 2

No, no, there is nothing in the world that can
be imagined in advance, not the slightest thing.
Everything is made up of so many unique
particulars that are impossible to foresee.

—RAINER MARIA RILKE,
from *The Notebooks of Malte Laurids Brigge*

Contents

Any Person Is the Only Self

On Recently Returned Books

I used to go to a public library almost weekly. It was the central branch in Denver, a sprawling building on the edge of downtown, near the capitol, the art museum, and the courthouse where I got married. I was always stopping in to pick up a row of holds, or to browse the new releases, or to wander the fiction stacks on the second floor, or to check out the little used-book shop near the rear entrance, which was open only at odd hours. But my favorite spot was a shelf near the borrower-services desk, marked with a sign reading RECENTLY RETURNED.

I noticed this shelf the first time I went into the library, shortly after moving to the city, to open an account. It held a few dozen books—about as many as you'd see on a table at the front of a bookstore, where the books have earned prominence by way of being new and important, bestsellers, or staff favorites. But the books on this shelf weren't recommended by anyone. There was no implication they were vetted or approved by a librarian or even the last borrower. That's what amazed me. They were just random books.

At this library, the collection is spread out over multiple floors. It was too big to browse very effectively, especially when I didn't have a genre or subject in mind. The recently

returned shelf limited my choices, presenting a cross section of all removable parts of the library. Sometimes, when
I was in a hurry, it was the only shelf I looked at. There
were art books and manga, self-help and philosophy, biographies and thrillers, the popular mixed up with the very
obscure. I liked how it reduced the scope of my options,
but without imposing any one person's taste or agenda upon
me, or the generalized taste of the masses suggested by
algorithms. The books on that shelf weren't being mar-
keted to me; they weren't omnipresent in my social media
feeds. They were often old and very often ugly. I came to
think of that shelf as an escape from hype. It was negative
hype. It was anti-curation.

Picking them up, I half expected the books to be warm,
like just-vacated seats. Some still contained the life detri-
tus of the last person to open them: makeshift bookmarks
with identifying information, boarding passes or receipts;
oil stains or flecks of melted chocolate (I also read while
eating); even drops of blood. An eyelash. Sometimes the
books made me itchy, and I would know the last borrower
had a dog. Sometimes there were clusters of related books
that must have been checked out by the same patron. These
books always conjured a borrower—a faceless but familiar
stranger. It was like getting to look at someone's nightstand.
It was everyone's nightstand, an average of all nightstands.
A manifest version of collective consciousness.

There were sometimes funny juxtapositions: a book of
dessert recipes called *Butter Celebrates!* right next to *The Miracle of Fasting.* A book called *Finding Masculinity* next to *Wicca
for One.* It's possible that someone on the staff was arranging
the books to amuse themselves. But I think the jokes would

appear spontaneously, even without purposeful intervention. Randomness is interesting. It's why professional poker players pay so much to see the flop. Suddenly your bad cards could get interesting, could turn into a straight or a flush draw. Suddenly you're glad you didn't fold.

I took books from that shelf I never would have sought out otherwise—once, a Rachael Ray book I probably grabbed on impulse because I was hungry. I don't think of myself as a Rachael Ray person. It turned out not to be a cookbook exactly, but a kind of food diary recording her meals every day for a year, full of nonprofessional snapshots, badly lit and poignantly mediocre: the simple dishes she cooks for her husband over and over, her mother's requests on holidays, multiple variations on deviled eggs. She doesn't describe it this way, but it demonstrates a sort of recursive model for cooking, where bits of yesterday's dinner end up in tonight's, and bits of tonight's in tomorrow's, and so on— like you're giving your food a sense of memory. I read it twice before returning it, and years later, I still think about it. Food is so personal. Anything you do every day—that's your life.

On another occasion, I found an orange paperback called *What Should We Be Worried About?*, in which scientists and scholars pontificate on threats to human existence: Which are the most urgent, the worst of our worries? I never read the book, but I kept it around for months, letting it autorenew, looking at the spine and sort of meditating on the title: *What* should *we be worried about?* Then it was due, and I took it back.

———

In the early weeks of lockdown, the spring of 2020, the library was closed—not that we would have gone in if it were open. My husband and I were probably excessively cautious about indoor spaces, where we'd have to breathe the same air as strangers. I remember missing the library intensely during that time. I missed the abundance of free reading material, the low commitment of books I could flip through once and never look at again. I also missed the strangers, the not-quite-strangers who live in your city, the ones you never meet but repeatedly see.

I decided I would buy almost no books that year, and instead try to read the many books in our own library I hadn't gotten to yet. Our apartment in Denver had a long wall with no doors or windows, which we filled with a row of seven dark Billy bookcases from IKEA. I was proud of that wall of books, and anyone who entered our apartment always commented on its beauty. Every single maintenance guy who came to fix our toilet or replace an appliance over ten years remarked on those shelves.

We often sold books, but new ones came in, and the shelves were always at full capacity. There was a row of books on the very top of the shelves too, mostly reference texts and art books and anthologies. The rest was a mix of fiction and nonfiction arranged in alphabetical order by author. I'm always surprised when writers have no organizational system for their books, or arrange them by color. Under our system, I can go to our shelves to see if we have a book John has acquired without my knowledge, or owned since before we met, without having to know what it looks like. But also, I prefer the look of spines in random color patterns. This randomness looks beautiful to me, an aesthetic in itself.

It occurs to me now that I should have asked John to re-create the serendipity effect of the library by pulling a selection of books off our own shelves for me. It would have been akin to the home version of *Chopped* we sometimes play, when he brings home a "basket" of four surprise ingredients I have to incorporate into dinner. Once it was pork chops, radishes, arugula, and marmalade. Pork chops are fine, but I never buy them, and I don't like marmalade. Yet it was a good dinner. I sautéed half the radishes in butter, and put the others in a salad. I used the marmalade to make a vinaigrette.

I had already been working from home for years, but that March, John was still teaching in person, so every time he left the house he stopped for more groceries. We wanted a full freezer. One Monday he got up early and went to Whole Foods right when it opened. He came back visibly shaken by the experience, the atmosphere of panic. The store was so crowded people kept bumping into him, so he immediately threw all his clothes in the wash and got in the shower. We didn't really know how the virus spread yet. Unpacking the groceries, I felt like crying. It was so much like our game. The store had been cleaned out of staples, so the bags were a haphazard mix of exotic treats—bison steaks, miso broth, fresh halibut. He had thought to get tomato paste and a backup jar of mayonnaise. The only olive oil they had looked expensive, something Spanish, a green bottle with a cork. We eventually found other oil, so I used the green bottle sparingly. It took on a mysterious significance, reminding me always of that precipice in time when the future felt unusually unknowable. I kept it long after it was empty, and couldn't bring myself to throw it away until we moved.

Back then, cooking was the only time I felt normal. I made a curry with the halibut, and topped it with the last of a bunch of fresh mint we had in the fridge. The next night I made pork chops—so like our game!—with grits and braised kale, and the following night I made a hash with the leftover pork. It was like a little puzzle, figuring out what to cook for dinner—starting with whatever was most perishable, limiting what I took from the freezer or pantry, incorporating scraps or bits of sauce from previous meals. Recursively.

I often thought about how much of "normal life" I had taken for granted. Before, when I had needed something, or simply wanted it, I could just go out and get it. I had never appreciated that my routines weren't dangerous. I know this thought is not original—in fact it strikes me as profoundly unoriginal. In fact it seemed like everyone I knew was having all the same feelings in the same order. First, I feared my parents wouldn't take the risk of the virus seriously enough. I started talking to them every day—pressuring my father, an internist, to close his office—and after a few weeks, a little less often, when we ran out of things to say. Nothing new was happening. I watched a movie on my laptop, hyperaware of how often the characters touched their own faces. I had an anxiety dream that I'd accidentally gone to a party. I had a wish-fulfillment dream about grocery shopping, filling my cart with specialty meats and good olives at the deli. I went on a walk and felt like I was playing a live-action video game, trying to stay six feet away from other walkers and joggers at all times, while also trying not to get hit by a car. When I told my friends these things, or shared any recent observation or impression at all, they always said, *Me too!* or, *Exact same.* We were all struggling to focus on reading and work. We were having the same dreams.

Over the course of that first month, I read for longer and longer stretches, as though building my strength back up after an injury. When I couldn't read and wasn't working or sleeping, I chain-smoked crosswords, a kind of verbal solitaire that made a decent substitute for human conversation. One night I read for hours without looking at my phone. By mid-April, I felt that my reading comprehension and concentration were getting back to normal. When I called my best friend, who lived in Brooklyn with her husband and toddler, she too was feeling better; she'd reached a semi-Zen plane of acceptance. Same feelings, same order. It was as if our interior lives that once felt so variegated, so individual, were just the result of having slightly different experiences at different times. We were not as unique as we thought—or we needed more input, more life in our lives, to make it so.

The COVID pandemic has coincided nearly exactly with my forties, making it hard to account for changes. Which is the true cause—of certain new anxieties, of new types of pain in my back—my age or this widespread collapse, this near-constant threat? Another change is less change—less welcome change, in any case. I meet fewer people; I seem to have less time to try new things. I often think about taking a class, but never do it. I think about how varied my friends were in college, with their many different interests. They've gone on to be lawyers or physicists, architects or programmers. Now almost all my friends are writers.

I always thought the term "midlife crisis" was quaint, but now that I'm here, in the middle of my life, I feel the full force of the word "crisis." Its Grecian drama. The Germans have a good word for it too: *Torschlusspanik*, or "shut-door panic"—"fear of being on the wrong side of a closing gate." That reminds me of Virginia Woolf's remark in her journal, after attending a friend's funeral: "Of course I shall lie there too before that gate and slide in." You know all your life that you're going to die, but you don't *really* know it, until you cross that fold. It feels like a crisis of faith, but faith in what? Not God, not in my case. Perhaps an unspoken belief I hadn't realized I needed to function, an unexamined assumption that my life would continue getting *better*. That making good choices would lead to more freedom. I hadn't known, really known, that there would be fewer choices. The belief depends on choices, on multiple paths with unpredictable end points. On still-open gates. That is faith, isn't it? Belief in what you can't know? Chance is a kind of hope.

In the summer of 2021, my mother and John's father, by misfortunate coincidence, were both hospitalized with sepsis—my mother in Texas, my father-in-law in Connecticut. For a week I was prepared to fly to one or the other. We clung to our phones, waiting for news that would force a decision. ("Crisis" has its origin in medical settings—the turning point in an illness.) At the end of that week, my mother went home, exhausted but alive. It's the kind of condition that can weaken you forever. My father-in-law was eventually transferred to a different facility, but he never made it home. He died that fall. I remembered the year that my mother's mother and John's father's mother, our last surviving grandparents, both left us, in their nineties. Until they were dead, it hadn't really seemed possible that our parents could die too—rather, that they would die too. This was an illusion—as if things would all happen in order. After John's father's death, we ourselves felt more fragile.

There is the terror of too much uncertainty, and then there is the horror of knowing too much. The imagined versus the actual. I have a friend whose therapist tells him, "You know too much to be happy"—meaning, it's too hard to live when you believe you can see how the rest of your life will play out. That may be what I miss most about youth: unknowing without fear. The future felt longer, yes—I was so rich with time, I could waste as much as I wanted—but not only longer. It was blanker.

We spent all our years in Denver in the same apartment, because every time our lease renewal came up, we'd consider the effort of moving and decide to stay put. By the spring of 2022, the third year of the pandemic, we were finally ready to do the work. We packed all our things, eighty or ninety boxes of books, and moved back to New England, temporarily settling in John's hometown. We hoped it might be our last big move. I had doubts and regrets, and people could tell, but I told them, "Change is good." I don't actually think that all change is good. That would be delusional. I suppose I meant, change might be good. Good change is possible.

There's a used bookstore not far from John's childhood home, called the Book Barn, where we've spent many hours and dollars. It's a chain of old buildings, with little garden paths between, a little pen with some goats you can feed. The best part, especially when the weather is nice, are the outdoor shelves of new arrivals, just behind the desk where you bring books to sell. The new arrivals aren't in any order yet, and the staff buys a lot of books—new books and old books, classics and trash. They've often been sold and re-sold. The pages are often foxed. It's a very lucky bookstore. I almost always find something I've been looking for, and it feels especially lucky when it's among the new arrivals, like I've come just in time.

Sometimes John goes to the bookstore alone and brings home something he thinks I might like, some book I've never heard of, a four-dollar risk, and it makes me happy. I need that in my life. I need randomness to be happy.

The Stupid Classics Book Club

At a party several years ago, John and I and two friends decided to start up a "Stupid Classics Book Club." It began as a joke, and then struck us as a genuinely good idea. The project of this book club would be to read all the corny stuff from the canon that we really should have read in school but never had. I pulled out a notebook, and we spent the next hour and a half in a corner, coming up with a list of stupid classics. As we went along, we had to figure out exactly what we meant by "stupid." We did not mean "lacking in intelligence," or "bad." For me, "stupid" meant relatively short, accessible enough to be on a high school syllabus, and probably rehashed into cliché over time by multiple film adaptations and *Simpsons* episodes. The quintessential example was *Dr. Jekyll and Mr. Hyde.* Anything too long or serious—Proust, *Middlemarch*—was excluded from the list, even if we all wanted to read it, due to failing those criteria. We did not assume any of the classics would actually be stupid.

We were wrong on that last count. The first book we chose to read was *Fahrenheit 451.* We'd all read some Ray Bradbury as kids, but not this one. A couple of weeks later, when my friend Mike texted to say he had almost finished it, I texted back, "No spoilers." He responded with a semi-spoiler: "It's . . . good for this book club." I opened it up and read the first page:

> It was a pleasure to burn.
>
> It was a special pleasure to see things eaten, to see things blackened and *changed*. With the brass nozzle in his fists, with this great python spitting its venomous kerosene upon the world, the blood pounded in his head, and his hands were the hands of some amazing conductor playing all the symphonies of blazing and burning to bring down the tatters and charcoal ruins of history. With his symbolic helmet numbered 451 on his stolid head, and his eyes all orange flame with the thought of what came next, he flicked the igniter and the house jumped up in a gorging fire that burned the evening sky red and yellow and black.

I'm not *always* against laying it on thick, but I knew from the first sentence that I wasn't going to like this. After thirty or forty pages, I texted Mike: "This book is so dumb it should be burned." In the end, all four of us hated it. You might think the book's central message (censorship is bad) is inherently noble, but not quite: Bradbury wrote it in response to his own critics, critics who had pointed out that his work was racist, sexist, and xenophobic. That motivation is present in the text. It's defensive and reactionary. But just in case you missed it, Bradbury spelled it out in a coda to the book he wrote in 1979:

> Fire Captain Beatty, in my novel *Fahrenheit 451*, described how the books were burned first by the mi-

norities, each ripping a page or a paragraph from this book, then that, until the day came when the books were empty and the minds shut and the library closed forever.

In Bradbury's view of the universe, white men wrote good and important books, while "the minorities" and "women's libbers" tried to censor them. Except for one manic pixie dream girl who shakes Montag out of his complacency and is swiftly killed off (I missed her when she was gone), all the women in *Fahrenheit 451* are zombie harpies. Montag eventually joins a band of men who have memorized the great books, the only way to save them from burning: "We are all bits and pieces of history and literature and international law, Byron, Tom Paine, Machiavelli or Christ, it's here." They are the heroes protecting the Western canon from destruction by cultural criticism. To be clear, I'm not in *favor* of censoring books, even ones I find morally repugnant. But I'm puzzled by Bradbury's argument (again, from the coda) that "it is a mad world and it will get madder if we allow the minorities, be they dwarf or giant, orangutan or dolphin, nuclear-head or water-conservationist, pro-computerologist or Neo-Luddite, simpleton or sage, to interfere with aesthetics." (Has a dolphin been a censor? If anything, aren't we censoring dolphins?) In terms of the aesthetics, it's a sloppy, silly, heavy-handed, humorless book. Bradbury wrote the first draft as a short story in nine days, then expanded the story to novel length in another nine. You can tell. We didn't have a fireplace, but after the book club met, we threw our cheap paperback copy in the trash.

For our next pick, the members of the SCBC all agreed we wanted something we knew would be good. We went with *Frankenstein*. I was amazed by how different the novel was from my received ideas about it. I had not expected the monster to be so articulate, or to have read *The Sorrows of Young Werther* (my reaction bordered on jealousy—*I* haven't even read that!). I could also never quite decide how to picture him. If I've seen a movie version of a book before I read it, I inevitably picture the actors from the movie; I saw and heard Anthony Hopkins in my head while reading *The Remains of the Day*, though I've never seen the movie, just the trailers. But I didn't picture Boris Karloff or the boxy, bolted head of Halloween masks. Mary Shelley's description of the creature didn't match: "His hair was of a lustrous black, and flowing; his teeth of a pearly whiteness." Victor Frankenstein "had selected his features as beautiful"—but is appalled at the uncanny, living result. Once he escapes, the monster bounds around the snowy Alps like a yeti, so I pictured something hirsute, an Edward Gorey drawing, with perfectly round yellow eyes. The one thing I thought I knew, the monster's physicality, I had gotten wrong. Almost everything about the book defied my expectations.

Our third selection was my definitive "stupid classic": *Strange Case of Dr. Jekyll and Mr. Hyde*. From the first sentence, I was delighted: "Mr. Utterson the lawyer was a man of a rugged countenance that was never lighted by a smile; cold, scanty and embarrassed in discourse; backward in sentiment; lean, long, dusty, dreary and yet somehow lovable." I laughed out loud; it's like a better, funnier version of the not-beautiful-woman-who-is-still-somehow-beautiful. I loved the next sentence too: "At friendly meetings, and when the wine was to his taste, something eminently human beaconed from his eye; something indeed which never found its way into his talk, but which spoke not only in these silent symbols of the after-dinner face, but more often and loudly in the acts of his life." Montag's "symbolic helmet" is as terrible (I get that it's a symbol, thanks) as "silent symbols of the after-dinner face" is great. I read on mostly for the prose, which is full of these anti-clichés, these totally surprising phrases: one man is described as "about as emotional as a bagpipe" (I was not sure, at first, if this meant very emotional or not emotional at all); another as having "a kind of black, sneering coolness . . . but carrying it off, sir, really like Satan." Two old friends are described as "thorough respecters of themselves and of each other." A woman's face betrays a "flash of odious joy." I found the writing hilarious, appropriately full of contradictions, but also beautiful:

> It was by this time about nine in the morning, and the first fog of the season. A great chocolate-coloured pall lowered over heaven, but the wind was continually charging and routing these embattled vapours; so that as the cab crawled from street to street, Mr. Utterson beheld a marvellous number of degrees and hues of twilight; for here it would be dark like the back-end of evening; and there would be a glow of a rich, lurid brown, like the light of some strange conflagration; and here, for a moment, the fog would be quite broken up, and a haggard shaft of daylight would glance in between the swirling wreaths.

"Chocolate-coloured pall," "the back-end of evening"—
"rich, lurid brown"! How much more arresting than Bradbury's orange flames.

I told a friend at the time that I was enjoying the writing
a lot, but didn't really care about the story per se, the whole
"devil inside" thing. This was before I got to the last twenty
pages, the chapter titled "Henry Jekyll's Full Statement
of the Case." (I generally don't think chapters in novels
need titles or even numbers, unless they are as wonderful
as Robert Louis Stevenson's—"Story of the Door," "Incident at the Window"—or E. M. Forster's—"Music, Violets,
and the Letter 'S.'") Up to that point, the plot had pretty
much aligned with the version I'd absorbed through cultural references and cartoons: the doctor transforms into
a smaller, uglier, more evil person after drinking a magic
potion in his laboratory. In this changed form he's free to
roam about doing his sinister deeds; he can always change
back and be innocent again. In this last chapter, Jekyll explains why he began his experiments. From youth he'd been
aware of "a profound duplicity of life." He was "in no sense
a hypocrite," he says, doing good actions while thinking
dark thoughts. Rather, "both sides" were real: "I was rad-
ically both." As Mr. Hyde, he discovers, he can give himself over completely to darkness: "I knew myself, at the first
breath of this new life, to be more wicked, tenfold more
wicked, sold a slave to my original evil; and the thought,
in that moment, braced and delighted me like wine." He is
completely free as Hyde, he believes, and completely free of
consequence: "Think of it—I did not even exist!"

Then comes a moment that stunned me: One night
Jekyll turns in late and wakes in the morning with "odd

sensations." Nothing in his room looks amiss, yet "something still kept insisting that I was not where I was, that I had not wakened where I seemed to be." He has the feeling he should not be in his own room, with its "decent furniture and tall proportions," all present and accounted for, but in the dingy "little room in Soho" where he sometimes sleeps as Hyde. The displacement is not in the room but in his body—he looks down and sees not the "large, firm, white and comely" hand of Jekyll but the "corded," "knuckly," "dusky" hand of Hyde. He has gone to bed good and woken evil.

Initially, Jekyll explains, the more difficult part of the transformation had been going from Jekyll to Hyde, but the more he transformed, the more this reversed: "I was slowly losing hold of my original and better self, and becoming slowly incorporated with my second and worse." Eventually he can't sleep at all without spontaneously converting: "If I slept, or even dozed for a moment in my chair, it was always as Hyde that I awakened." He cannot escape Hyde because Hyde no longer needs the potion, only Jekyll does, and Jekyll has run out of supplies. He *is* Hyde now, the evil "knit to him closer than a wife, closer than an eye."

I had no inkling of this part of the story, which now seems to me infinitely richer and more complex than I'd imagined—it's no longer simply about good versus evil, but any kind of unwanted or frightening change. I can read the final pages, which Jekyll narrates from the knowledge that it's his last chance to "think his own thoughts or see his own face," as a metaphor for aging or addiction or illness, the approach of death as a loss of the self—Jekyll's last moments as moments of lucidity where you recognize yourself as you are and remember the self that is disappearing, and can fathom the gap in between. The biographical note in my copy of *Jekyll and Hyde* tells me Stevenson died suddenly of a cerebral hemorrhage at the age of forty-four. I've read this part over and over: "The kindly author went down to the cellar to fetch a bottle of his favorite burgundy, uncorked it in the kitchen, abruptly cried out to his wife, 'What's the matter with me, what is this strangeness, *has my face changed?*'— and fell to the floor." It was his last transformation.

"You think you know, but you have no idea." That's the catchphrase for an old MTV show called *Diary* that I've seen exactly once. In that episode, from 2004, we follow Lindsay Lohan around for a day to see what her life is supposedly really like. Every time it cuts back from commercial, we hear Lohan saying the catchphrase. In my head it's the catchphrase for the Stupid Classics Book Club too. I thought I knew, but I had no idea. It was trendy for a while to publish lists of classics that "you don't have to read." In 2018, *GQ* named twenty-one books, including *The Adventures of Huckleberry Finn*, *Gulliver's Travels*, and the Bible, that "you don't have to read," with suggestions for what you should read instead. *Lit Hub* published a list of "10 Books to Read by Living Women (Instead of These 10 by Dead Men)." Since when is it poor form to die? I find these lists incredibly tiresome. Of course, you don't *have* to read anything. Some books will be insurmountably boring or make you deeply unhappy; there just isn't enough time. But if you want to speak or write knowledgeably about them, you really do have to read them. You can't just assume you know what they're like. I'm glad I read *Fahrenheit 451* even though

I despised it. Now I know exactly *how* it's bad, and I can hate it for the right reasons.

When I was younger, as a teenager and in my twenties, I often took for granted that "good art" was good—I was if anything overly trusting of authority—but I didn't take the time to actually experience that art's goodness for myself. The older I get, the more likely I am to think, *That's underrated*, about stuff that's completely established canon. (Sylvia Plath? Underrated! Led Zeppelin? Underrated!) It's not that these artists don't get enough attention; it's more that when something good is widely appreciated, we forget to take it seriously. We don't think it needs us. Or popularity itself makes art feel like a joke; we assume if it's famous, it must be obvious. In high school I wasn't impressed by the boys who owned Led Zeppelin albums (my friend Catherine might say they weren't "rising to the challenge of modernity"), so I didn't pay attention to Led Zeppelin. Now I listen to Led Zeppelin and think, *Excuse me, this fucking rules.*

On the first day of April one year, I felt an itch for some vernal ritual, some formal celebration of National Poetry Month and spring, though spring is my least favorite season. *The Waste Land* seemed just the thing, so I found a recording of T. S. Eliot reading the poem on YouTube and played it on a loop all morning like background music. It sounded so good, I opened the poem in a browser tab and vowed to keep it open all month, to dip into at random, whenever I wanted some gorgeous, contextless language. I first read *The Waste Land* in college, but I felt like I had never really read it—the way my instructors talked about it, I just assumed I wouldn't understand it, so I didn't bother trying.

I'm sure they meant well, intending to prepare us for the difficulty, but instead they scared us off. I now feel lied to, like they just wanted to keep *The Waste Land* for themselves. The back of the copy I bought at my college bookstore pulls the same trick, deepening its aura of obscurity: "When *The Waste Land* was published in 1922, initial reaction to the poem was decidedly negative. Critics attacked the poem's 'kaleidoscopic' design, and nearly everyone disagreed furiously about its meaning. The poem was even rumored to be a hoax." Can a poem be a hoax? John Ashbery used to show his classes unlabeled poems by Ern Malley—the invention of two Australian writers who hated modernist poetry— and Geoffrey Hill—an actual modernist poet—and have them guess which one was the spoof. They were right about half the time, because, of course, they were only guessing. Ashbery liked the fake poems, which were designed to be confusing. But poems that are not a little confusing have no mystery. "I am still / the black swan of trespass"—that's Malley, but could as easily be Hart Crane. Maybe all good poems are a bit of a hoax, or at least a bit of an accident—we can't *control* if they're good.

When reading Shakespeare, you can be pretty sure that any familiar phrases originated with him. This isn't quite so with *The Waste Land*. Many of Eliot's lines are famous on their own, but the text is so allusive, you might recognize a line from its source material instead—take "hypocrite lecteur!—mon semblable,—mon frère!" It's the last line of Eliot's first section, "The Burial of the Dead," and the last line of Baudelaire's preface to *Fleurs du mal*. Another reference to *Fleurs du mal* in "The Burial of the Dead" is less obvious: line 60, "Unreal City." Eliot's line note is

"Cf. Baudelaire: 'Fourmillante cité, cité pleine de rêves.'" It's not quite a translation of the line, more of a shorthand for it. Reading *The Waste Land* again recently, the phrase reminded me of something, but what? Not Baudelaire. Was it reminding me of itself, the first time I read it many years ago? No, it came to me—"unreal city" is a bit of a verse from an Okkervil River song called "Maine Island Lovers," on an album released in 2003, which I listened to obsessively in grad school, when I was living in a tiny apartment in Boston in a record year for snow.

This is why it's worth reading the classics—to spend enough time with a text that a reference to it isn't just outside you, but connected to your intimate experience of the text and all the other texts it connects to. Sometimes, lately, I get a glistening feeling that references, which are often, in any case, unintentional, are not one-way but reciprocal, that Eliot is referencing the Okkervil River song as much as the other way around. In the right mood, reading *The Waste Land*, I can feel unhooked from time, like Proust's narrator of *Swann's Way* dozing in his "magic" chair—the poem seems to allude both backward and forward, to reference the future.

Weird Time in *Frankenstein*

In her short nonfiction book *Ongoingness*, a single long, fragmentary essay, Sarah Manguso writes a meditative exegesis on her own diary, a document nearing a million words, which she added to daily, obsessively, for twenty-five years. This archival practice had felt like a necessity, a hedge against potential failures of memory, and the only way to process the onslaught of time: "I couldn't face the end of a day without a record of everything that had ever happened." It started when she was a teenager. She went to an art opening with a friend, drank wine from a plastic cup, looked at paintings—"It was all too much," the moment was "too full." She wouldn't have time to "recover" from the beauty of the day, she realized, since tomorrow would offer only *more* experience: "There should be extra days, buffer days, between the real days." (I've often thought there should be a little buffer between months, a transition period: a monthend.)

When Manguso became a mother, this anxious relationship to time changed:

> In my experience nursing is waiting. The mother becomes the background against which the baby lives, becomes time.

I used to exist against the continuity of time. Then I became the baby's continuity, a background of ongoing time for him to live against.

She stopped worrying so much about "lost memories"—being pregnant makes you forgetful, and when you have a small baby most days feel the same. But aging also changes us; we've moved further to the right on the timeline of our lives (that's how I picture it, like a side-scrolling video game), a line whose end point is death. At some point you can assume there's more time behind than ahead. Manguso mentions reading an essay by a ninety-year-old writer, the last thing he ever published, that issued a "terrible warning," in her words. She paraphrases the warning and does not name the writer, so I googled a few vague words and was surprised to find the essay right away: "Nearing 90," by William Maxwell.

"I am not—I think I am not—afraid of dying," Maxwell writes:

When I was 17 I worked on a farm in southern Wisconsin . . . The farm had come down in that family through several generations, to a woman who was so alive that everything and everybody seemed to revolve around her personality. She lived well into her 90's and then one day told her oldest daughter that she didn't want to live anymore, that she was tired.

This remark, he writes, "reconciled me to my own inevitable extinction." He has few regrets, and many happy memories, but if he wanders too deep into nostalgic reveries, they can keep him up all night. This is the warning Manguso refers to: the past can act as a trap. Maxwell adds, "I have liked remembering almost as much as I have liked living"— a thought I find beautiful and comforting. With so little to look forward to—Maxwell died at ninety-one—he took solace in looking back. Manguso, for her part, is finally able to take solace in forgetting: as time piles up, she loses access to specific moments, but begins to accept that life is ongoing, not discrete but continuous. It's more and more and more until it's over.

Because I had just read *Ongoingness*, when I started reading *Frankenstein*, I was thinking about time. (Well, I am always thinking about time.) Time is weird in *Frankenstein*, in part because of the nested narratives. First there's the epistolary framing narrative, the letters that Captain Walton writes to his sister on his voyage toward the North Pole. He and his crew rescue a man at sea, a man who turns out to be Victor Frankenstein. Victor then takes over the narrative, basically telling (the captain, but also us) his life story starting from birth. We get to the monster part in Chapter V. After many months of self-seclusion, subsumed in his studies of "natural philosophy," chemistry, and other dark arts, "on a dreary night of November," Frankenstein brings his gruesome humanoid to life. His fascination with this project instantly dissolves: "The beauty of the dream vanished, and breathless horror and disgust filled my heart." He runs from his creation to his bedroom and, unbelievably, tries to go to sleep, and, unbelievably, succeeds, only to be woken by the monster peeking in through his bedcurtains, like the Ghost of Christmas Past. Again Victor runs away, this time out into the courtyard. By morning, the monster is gone. Then something like two years go by with no monster in sight; he's on Frankenstein's mind, but he's not in the story.

We meet the monster again in Chapter X. Frankenstein's young brother has been murdered, and their beloved servant girl framed for it and executed. Victor is sure his creation is to blame. He's been wandering around, gazing at the Alps, the "glorious presence-chamber of imperial Nature," these "sublime and magnificent scenes" providing modest consolation to his suffering. And suddenly there is the monster, "the wretch." Victor goes off: "Do you dare approach me? . . . Begone, vile insect!" The "daemon" responds quite calmly, and in high formal register: "I expected this reception . . . All men hate the wretched; how, then, must I be hated, who am miserable beyond all living things!"

Then another embedded narrative begins; the "abhorred devil" takes Frankenstein back to his "hut upon the mountain" and tells his own tale. We learn, in the monster's words, what he's been doing all this time—taking shelter in a hovel behind a cottage and observing the family inside through cracks in the walls. From this poor, compassionate family—the father is blind—he learns something of humanity, and language; he learns even more from a "leathern portmanteau" he finds that contains some books, among them *Paradise Lost* and "*Sorrows of Werter*"! (Never mind how he learns to read; we don't even know why he's alive.) Like Napoleon and half of Europe in the late eighteenth century, Frankenstein's monster gets a touch of Werther Fever: "I thought Werter himself a more divine being than

I had ever beheld or imagined; his character contained no pretension, but it sunk deep." Werther's suicide causes him to weep, "without precisely understanding it."

Because of this nonlinear storytelling, we're left to puzzle out just what Victor was up to during his monster's intellectual coming of age. It's tricky in part because the emotional texture of their experiences was different. The monster's years feel richer, thus longer, to the reader; they held more joy. But from inside the experience, Victor's years full of fear and regret would surely have felt longer than the monster's happy ones; pain elongates time. On the other (other) hand, these were the first two years of the monster's existence; time is elongated in childhood in part because each day accounts for such a large proportion of one's lifetime so far. Birthdays and holidays feel more significant when you've lived through fewer of them, when from your own perspective they are much further apart. There's also a metabolic theory—because children's hearts beat faster, their bodies are clocking more time in a day than adults' bodies do. More heartbeats mean more perceived time. Would this apply to Frankenstein's monster? Was the monster born a child, or just naive? Maybe his love for the cottagers, and literature, quickened his pulse.

Can there be true simultaneity in fiction? In what sense do narratives that unspool at different times "happen" at the same time? Some of Shakespeare's plays seem to operate on two contradictory timescales, a phenomenon critics have dubbed "double time." But then, there's no true simultaneity in the real world either. Here's Wikipedia's enchanting ur-voice on the relativity of simultaneity: "According to the special theory of relativity introduced by Albert Einstein, it is impossible to say in an *absolute* sense that two distinct events occur at the same time if those events are separated in space." From some perspectives, the events are simultaneous, but from others they are not, and no perspective has inherent primacy over another. (At one point, the monster quotes from Percy Shelley's poem "Mutability," which makes no sense at all, since the narrative takes place before the poem was written.)

The novel's chronology is further complicated by the fact that Mary Shelley wrote the first version before her husband Percy's death by drowning in 1822, but the version we commonly read now is a revision first published in 1831. Mary's mother, the radical feminist Mary Wollstonecraft, died ten days after her daughter was born. When the author of *Frankenstein* was sixteen, she met Percy Shelley, who was already married, but they ran away together anyway, which earned her the same bad sexual reputation that her mother had had. In a biographical introduction to a critical edition of the novel, Johanna M. Smith writes that Mary Shelley "never entirely escaped the social effects of her early indiscretion," "even though she married Percy in 1816, within a month of his wife Harriet's suicide"—as if this latter move was the soul of discretion. Mary and Percy weren't destined for happiness—three of their four children died very young, and in 1822 she had a miscarriage. Then, on July 8, Percy died in a shipwreck. Famously, when his body washed up on the shore, his face unrecognizable, he had a book of poems by Keats in his breast pocket. His clothes must have been very close-fitting.

In the final paragraph of her introduction to the 1831 edition, Shelley claims to have changed very little:

> I will add but one word as to the alterations I have made. They are principally those of style. I have changed no portion of the story, nor introduced any new ideas or circumstances. I have mended the language where it was so bald as to interfere with the interest of the narrative; and these changes occur almost exclusively in the beginning of the first volume. Throughout they are entirely confined to such parts as are mere adjuncts to the story, leaving the core and substance of it untouched.

I have not read the original 1818 version, but according to Anne K. Mellor's biography of Mary Shelley, the two versions *are* quite different, because Shelley's worldview had changed. Her layers of grief—their dear friend Lord Byron died two years after Percy, from what was likely septic fever—combined with her "financially straightened circumstances and her guilt-ridden and unshakeable despair" to convince her "that human events are decided not by personal choice or free will but by material forces beyond our control." Shelley's "new vision of nature's relationship to humanity is registered in the novel itself," Mellor writes. The characters become pawns of fate; they can't quite be blamed for destroying their own lives: "In 1818 Victor Frankenstein possessed free will or the capacity for meaningful moral choice . . . In 1831 such choice is denied to him."

I wondered if Shelley's misfortunes in the 1820s were

also responsible for the novel's obsession with loneliness. Everyone in the story, in particular the three men—if the monster can be called a man—who take control of the narrative in turn, longs desperately for companionship. Walton writes, in his second letter posted from Archangel, a Russian port on the White Sea: "I have one want which I have never yet been able to satisfy, and the absence of the object of which I now feel as a most severe evil, I have no friend, Margaret . . . You may deem me romantic, my dear sister, but I bitterly feel the want of a friend." He does not expect to find one on the ocean, but he does, in Victor Frankenstein. Frankenstein left his lifelong friends behind to attend university; it may be his isolation that leads him astray. The monster's loneliness is especially keen. He calls the poor cottagers his friends, although they're ignorant of his existence: "When they were unhappy, I felt depressed; when they rejoiced, I sympathized in their joys. I saw few human beings besides them, and if any other happened to enter the cottage, their harsh manners and rude gait only enhanced to me the superior accomplishments of my friends." When he works up the courage to approach them, they cower in fear and chase him off. The monster realizes he is doomed to solitude, people will never accept him; so he demands that his creator provide a companion for him, a girl-fiend, like Adam asking God for Eve. At first, moved, Victor agrees, but then decides in good conscience he can't and reneges. The monster gets revenge by killing all of Victor's friends, so he too must suffer alone.

Could Shelley have woven these themes in as part of her revision, to force her characters to suffer alone as she suffered? It doesn't appear so. The word "friend" appears 134

times in the 1831 version, and 131 times in the original edition. So mourning and loss were always part of the horror
in her horror story. It had come to her, as she describes in
the introduction she wrote in October of 1831, like a transmission and kept her awake: "When I placed my head on
my pillow, I did not sleep, nor could I be said to think. My
imagination, unbidden, possessed and guided me, gifting
the successive images that arose in my mind with a vivid-
ness far beyond the usual bounds of reverie." I think of her
lying there ("the dark *parquet*, the closed shutters, with the
moonlight struggling through") like William Maxwell in
a parallel insomnia, lost in his past. In the morning, she
transcribes "the grim terrors" of her "waking dream." She
envisions it as "a short tale," but Percy pushes her to "develop the idea at greater length." It becomes the story of her
life. *Frankenstein*, her "hideous progeny," was "the offspring
of happy days, when death and grief were but words, which
found no true echo in my heart." It's as though this conscious nightmare were a premonition.

Party Lit

In her 2008 review of Cecily von Ziegesar's Gossip Girl novels, Janet Malcolm quotes the eponymous narrator's "opening volley": "We all live in huge apartments with our own bedrooms and bathrooms and phone lines. We have unlimited access to money and booze and whatever else we want, and our parents are rarely home, so we have tons of privacy. We're smart, we've inherited classic good looks, we wear fantastic clothes, and we know how to party." How very direct. I'm a grown-up person, so I've never read the books, but on the CW show (*Gossip Girl here! Your one and only source into the scandalous lives of Manhattan's elite*") the actors playing these trust-fund teens aren't just classically good-looking; they seem like genetic impossibilities. Blake Lively is perfectly cast as the "incandescently beautiful," in Malcolm's words, Serena van der Woodsen. She's five feet ten and usually wearing heels. Heather Cocks and Jessica Morgan of the blog *Go Fug Yourself* used to call her "Boobs Legsly." Serena and her friends and enemies (there is often little distinction between the two) have not only lucked into the 1 percent, they are also having an unfair, possibly immoral amount of fun.

Classic party fiction is often, if not always, a kind of

wealth porn. When Emma Bovary arrives at La Vaubyes-
sard, the château of the marquis, for dinner and a ball,
the opulence blows her bourgeois mind: "The red claws
of the lobsters overhung the edges of the platters; large fruits
were piled on moss in openwork baskets; the quails wore
their feathers; coils of steam rose into the air; and, grave as
a judge in his silk stockings, knee breeches, white tie, and
jabot, the butler conveyed the platters." Party scenes are full
of these lists of foods and drinks and flowers, overloaded
sentences that embody abundance, the fulsome displays of
affluence. See Nick Carraway's first party at Jay Gatsby's:
"Every Friday five crates of oranges and lemons arrived
from a fruiterer in New York . . . On buffet tables, gar-
nished with glistening hors-d'oeuvre, spiced baked hams
crowded against salads of harlequin designs and pastry pigs
and turkeys bewitched to a dark gold." Was Flaubert among
the first to use these litanies—appalled by the excess? (Jane
Austen's balls are disappointingly devoid of visual detail, as
if the evidence of money was just assumed. The European
novel hadn't gotten to Balzacian realism yet.) A truly expensive party should feel otherworldly; the marquis's ball, by
putting Emma in "contact with wealth," leaves her utterly
changed. It makes "a hole in her life, like those great chasms
that a storm, in a single night, will sometimes open in the
mountains."

In Edith Wharton's *The House of Mirth*, the element of
unreality is achieved by the tableaux vivants, elaborate live
reenactments of Botticelli's *Primavera* and Tiepolo's *Ban-
quet of Cleopatra*. With their "happy disposal of lights and
the delusive interposition of layers of gauze," the tableaux

"give magic glimpses of the boundary world between fact and imagination." Lily Bart appears as *Mrs. Lloyd*, a Joshua Reynolds painting—the guests are titillated and a little shocked ("Deuced bold thing to show herself in that get-up," one says), so I initially pictured something more typically male-gazey than the actual portrait, not a woman reclining but standing up, fully dressed, and carving her husband's name in a tree. In any case, it casts the necessary spell to carry Lily and Lawrence Selden away from the party, "against the tide which was setting thither," past faces that "flowed by like the streaming images of sleep," so they can kiss and whisper of love. Classic parties often have a watery quality. Nick Carraway is surrounded by "swirls and eddies of people" he doesn't know. It's the wet, blurry view through the bottom of a glass.

In his review of *Making It* by Norman Podhoretz, James Wolcott mentions an after-party for a *Commentary* symposium where the critic Alfred Kazin "found himself in a bobbing sea of familiar faces." *Making It*, Podhoretz's memoir of his ascent to "fame" in the 1950s and '60s—he was the editor of *Commentary*, which earned him entry to the world of the literati—was widely reviled upon its first publication, according to legend. Wolcott calls it "a book that would live in notoriety, which at least beats total obscurity." I wanted to root for the memoir, as an underdog, until I read parts of it; its naked egotism really is embarrassing. The passage of interest to me describes the parties: "One met most of the same people—the family—at all these parties, but there was usually enough variation in the crowd to breed other invitations to other parties." Parties, like genes, exist to self-replicate. This partly explains why they all look the same. In Evelyn Waugh's *A Handful of Dust*, Brenda is pleased with a party because it is "exactly what she wished it to be, an accurate replica of all the best parties she had been to in the last year; the same band, the same supper and, above all, the same guests."

Parties also perform the all-important function of establishing and reinforcing hierarchies. "Parties were sometimes fun and sometimes not, but fun was beside the point," Podhoretz writes. "For me they always served as a barometer of the progress of my career." The day his *New Yorker* review of the new Nelson Algren comes out, he receives an invite to a fancy party by telegram. He attends shindigs hosted by Lillian Hellman and Philip Rahv and Mary McCarthy and "(at last!)" Hannah Arendt. *Making It* contains a brief and fairly innocuous description of one of Arendt's famous New Year's Eve parties, which so infuriated her that she stopped having them for a few years. Podhoretz, for a while at least, got mileage out of being insufferable: "Enemies are all to the good at an early stage of a critic's career, helping as they do to spread his name around." A *Vanity Fair* piece about "the party of the century," Truman Capote's Black and White Ball in 1966, quotes the Parisian aristocrat Étienne de Beaumont: "A party is never given for someone. It is given against someone."

The midcentury Manhattan party has its own mythology, captured most iconically perhaps in *Breakfast at Tiffany's*—the movie more than the novella. For all that's terrible about the movie (the book is racist too), the party scene is truly great. My favorite part is the shot of a woman standing in front of a big mirror with a gilt frame, laughing her ass off as she looks at her own reflection—she even touches the mirror lightly with her fingers, the way you'd touch a man's arm who made you laugh in conversation. Thirty seconds later, we cut back to the woman; she's still looking at herself, but now she's sobbing, her eye makeup streaked down her face. It captures that late-night razor's edge between chaotic fun and disaster. It's an improvement, I think, on the scene in the novella, a "stag party" where the only women in attendance are Holly Golightly and her six-foot-tall, jolie laide model friend Mag Wildwood ("She was a triumph over ugliness, so often more beguiling than real beauty"). You can see what lines inspired the woman with the mirror in the film. In the novella, while Mag is in the bathroom, Holly implies Mag has a venereal disease, and Mag returns to find all the men have gone cold. This pushes Mag over the edge: "Since gin to artifice bears the same relation as tears to mascara, her attractions at once dissembled." But the mirror woman in the movie isn't Mag, just a random partygoer—a party crowd is not individuated. As V. S. Pritchett writes of Emma Bovary, "Her periods of depravity do not single her out as an exceptionally deplorable human being, but rather make her part of the general, glum strangeness of the people around her." One bird in the tessellated wallpaper.

When I mentioned this scene to John, he said he always thought *Breakfast at Tiffany's* ripped off its parties from *The Recognitions*. He pulled our copy of the long (956 pages) William Gaddis novel off the shelf, located one of the scenes in question, and then told me four times to be careful with the

book (it's a first edition). The scene he bookmarked features
"a Village party":

> —I couldn't stand a Village party tonight. Could you
> Arny? They're always so quite ha . . .
> —Hideous, Herschel supplied.
> —I wasn't going to say that, silly. I was going to say
> harrowing. I couldn't stand one tonight, that special
> Village quality of inhuman ghastliness and dirt . . .
> Arny please don't have another drink.

There's a definite resemblance, the same forms of
pretension—money was important, but not as important as
social status or as taste. The apartments holding the parties were often small, and the cramped quarters help create
that sense of overfullness and festive abundance that requires more cash in larger rooms. Gaddis's Otto, a playwright, sees the party, any party, as an opportunity to be
seen: "Otto (thinking only of what it looked like to see Otto
entering a room) entered." Parties are about the collective
gaze, the ability to be seen from all angles, panoramically.
As someone blabs at Otto about Swinburne and "de Maupassant, Guy de Maupassant of course" ("It's like a mas-
querade isn't it . . . I feel so naked, don't you? among all
these frightfully masked people"), Otto looks around the
room "with restrained anticipation": "He was looking for
a mirror." He wanders through the party, compulsively
mentioning his latest play, which interests no one. There is
more of a sense of grim desperation than of excitement and
possibility. Guests vie for dominance and attention; there's
a bizarre, pervasive homophobic paranoia, like a version of

the Red Scare; the party ends when there's nothing left to drink. (In youth, parties are a setting for fun; they provide alcohol and drugs and a place to consume them. In adulthood, parties are not a means to getting drunk but an event you need to be drunk to endure.)

Otto is an introvert, but he's choosing to play an introvert too—his mask, his party persona. He retreats to the bookcase: "When among people he did not know, Otto often took down a book from which he could glance up and note the situation which he pretended to disdain." Here he can half read and half observe—and, he hopes, be observed observing. Possibly, Capote did lift this from Gaddis. Here's the unnamed narrator in *Breakfast*: "I was left abandoned by the bookshelves; of the books there, more than half were about horses, the rest baseball. Pretending an interest in *Horseflesh and How to Tell It* gave me sufficiently private opportunity for sizing Holly's friends." Or maybe by 1958, when the novella was published—Gaddis's novel came out in 1955—the bookshelf-hoverer was already a cliché, of party fiction if not actual parties, a detail as familiar as ice cubes clinking or dogs barking in the distance. If all parties resemble other parties, the way all party people resemble other party people, then all parties are intertextual, they all reference each other. Amusingly, John wrote a play on this particular cliché into his own first novel, in which a character pulls a book off a shelf at a party. The book is *The Recognitions*.

Where are the parties in nonfiction? A few years before I read it in full, I scanned Gore Vidal's memoir *Palimpsest* looking for dirt on Anaïs Nin's salons—Nin and Vidal were friends, kind of; he writes of even his closest friends with a measure of contempt—but while he alludes vaguely to parties, and describes hanging out with various literary celebrities in various cafés and bars, these encounters are usually mild, often a little awkward. The cover of our paperback of *A Moveable Feast* advertises tales of "the wild young years of the Lost Generation in Paris," but it's not a wild book. When Hemingway meets Scott Fitzgerald, you think the partying is about to get good, but Hemingway depicts Fitzgerald as a melancholy hypochondriac who can't hold his liquor: "Scott did not like the places nor the people and he had to drink more than he could drink." They go to Lyon together to retrieve a car Fitzgerald has left there, and Hemingway is annoyed that drinking literally all day while they drive across France in an open car in the rain should have any effect on his companion—Fitzgerald becomes convinced he's going to die of something called "congestion of the lungs" and keeps insisting that Hemingway take his temperature. Hemingway's solution is to order him double whiskeys. There are no parties qua parties. Even Podhoretz mentions them only in passing, as a way to drop some names. It must be that people don't remember real parties well enough to re-create them with any accuracy. There's too much missing information. Fictive parties evoke this sense of impaired time by impairing the narrative, with non sequiturs, snippets of nonsense conversation, continuity errors. It's often suddenly two a.m. Whole hours may go by in the space of a sentence, as in *A Handful of Dust*: "They drank a lot." Those four words are one paragraph, and contain so much.

In the last episode of *Gossip Girl*, everyone gets married—

more Shakespearean comedy than Whartonian tragedy. But most classic, post-Austen party fiction ends badly. Lily Bart OD's on her "sleeping draught," probably meant to be laudanum. There is more at stake at these parties than having a good time—they don't party because they are *happy*. John O'Hara's *Appointment in Samarra*, published in 1934, might be the most tragic of the bunch. It begins with a Christmas party in "the smoking room of the Lantenengo Country Club," which is "so crowded it did not seem as though another person could get in." The usuals are there ("the Whit Hofmans, the Julian Englishes, the Froggy Ogdens and so on"), interchangeable "terrible people" getting "gloriously drunk" on "drug store rye" ("It was not poisonous, and it got you tight, which was all that was required of it and all that could be said for it"). The fun ends when Julian English throws a highball in Harry Reilly's face. Over the next three days, self-destructive to the point of insanity, Julian stays trashed, trashes his marriage, then takes a bottle of Scotch and a package of cigarettes into the garage and starts the car. The following day, Caroline is wretched with grief—"a tunnel you had to go through, had to go through, had to go through, had to go through"—grief as a never-ending hangover.

I have noticed one of the symptoms of a bad hangover is guilt—you regret all the toxins you've consumed, of course, but also the things you've said and done while your inhibitions were lowered, your temper shortened. I think of the end of Gatsby's party, when "most of the remaining women were now having fights with men said to be their husbands." The neurologist Oliver Sacks called the guilt of a hangover "penitential depression." The guilt is there even when you can't remember much of what happened. An old friend used to text me in the morning after parties: *Did I do anything horrible last night?* I'd text back, *Of course not.* But how would I know if she had? I was poisoned too.

Proust and the Joy of Suffering

One evening after work, as I so often do, in the agitated state between finishing one novel and deciding on another, I scanned through our bookshelves for something new to read. I considered *Moby-Dick*, as I so often do, but only briefly. I have long felt I'm saving *Moby-Dick* for an unclear future experience, some contained and isolating context it deserves—a long sea voyage, my deathbed. There is also my aversion to long novels, which is partly, but not merely, a form of laziness—or if it is, at base, a laziness, I've redescribed it to myself as a phobia, a more glamorous pathology. I was thinking about this when my eye caught *In Search of Lost Time*, another novel people, especially writers, almost brag about not having read, as though admitting you haven't read Proust suggests you've read everything else. I pulled *Swann's Way* off the shelf, read the first paragraph, and was almost offended. Its obsessive attention to memory, time, the minutiae of experience as it occurs through thinking—it was not just good. It was exactly my kind of thing. Everyone says you should read Proust, of course, but no one had ever told me, specifically, that *I* should read Proust.

Over the next couple of nights I read the "Overture"

chapter. I had the sense, while reading Proust, that I was "reading Proust," having a packaged experience like a tour of the Louvre. When friends asked what I was reading, I said, "I'm reading Proust, actually," acknowledging the improbability. "Wow," said my friend Kathleen, who knows me well. "Do you think you'll finish it?" "I highly doubt it," I said. It was more readable than I'd expected, but it wasn't exactly light. That first paragraph was deceptive, in part by virtue of being a paragraph. Later I read that Proust hadn't wanted *In Search of Lost Time* to have paragraphs at all. He wanted it to appear as one volume, with no sections, chapters, or even margins, incredibly. It's as though he wanted it to be unreadable, more a gesture than a text.

That Friday night, I remember, John and I stayed in to read, but I was tired and didn't feel up for Proust. Instead I went back to the shelves in search of something short. (Short books don't make me think of death; I don't worry I'll die before I finish them.) I found *My Name Is Lucy Barton* by Elizabeth Strout, which is the kind of book you can tear through in a couple of hours, and I did, only afterward realizing that thematically, it is not unlike *Swann's Way*. Lucy Barton recalls a time when she was very sick and had to stay in the hospital for over two months. Her mother, whom she hasn't seen in years, comes to visit and stays in her room, sitting at the foot of Lucy's bed and rarely sleeping, only dozing in her chair. Their conversations are often disturbing—Lucy grew up in poverty, with an abusive father, and she is not sure how much her mother knows, remembers, or has willfully forgotten. Their talks stir up the sediment of their grim past, but they are also often joyful:

"I was so happy. Oh, I was happy speaking with my mother this way!"

The overture to *Swann's Way* revolves around a memory or series of memories—the narrator's difficulty going to sleep without the benediction of a kiss from his mother—so overwhelming they seem to encompass the whole of his childhood. These memories, amalgamated in a single scene, come back to him each time he falls asleep:

> For a long time afterwards, when I lay awake at night and revived old memories of Combray, I saw no more of it than this sort of luminous panel, sharply defined against a vague and shadowy background . . . the hall through which I would journey to the first step of that staircase, so painful to climb, which constituted, all by itself, the slender cone of this irregular pyramid; and, at the summit, my bedroom, with the little passage through whose glazed door Mamma would enter; in a word, seen always at the same evening hour, isolated from all its possible surroundings, detached and solitary against the dark background, the bare minimum of scenery necessary (like the décor one sees prescribed on the title-page of an old play, for its performance in the provinces) to the drama of my undressing; as though all Combray had consisted of but two floors joined by a slender staircase, and as though there had been no time there but seven o'clock at night.

One night, when the family has been entertaining M. Swann—on such occasions our narrator is routinely sent to bed without his kiss—the boy decides he simply cannot go without it, and contrives to summon his mother by a ruse. He sends a note via Françoise, the cook. The ruse fails. He knows he has already angered his parents—they consider the ritual a silly indulgence and do not wish to coddle his delicate nerves—but having gone this far, he is committed to self-destruction: "I had formed a resolution to abandon all attempts to go to sleep without seeing Mamma, had made up my mind to kiss her at all costs . . . the calm which succeeded my anguish filled me with an extraordinary exhilaration, no less than my sense of expectation, my thirst for and my fear of danger."

He waits in the hall for his mother to come up to bed, his heart throbbing "with terror and joy." She is shocked and tries to send him back to bed before his father sees him, but in an unexpected turn of events, an amoral whim, his father rules in the boy's favor, sending her in to stay with the child all night: "Go along with him then . . . you can see quite well that the child is unhappy. After all, we aren't gaolers." Alone at last with her he dissolves into sobs. The cook asks, "But, Madame, what is young master crying for?" "Why, Françoise, he doesn't know himself: it's his nerves." His mother cries a little too, and it seems to be a mutual admission, a giving up: they cannot scare the child out of his fear; he will be delicate forever. He knows this event is "a rare and artificial exception," it can never happen again: "To-morrow night my anguish would return and Mamma would not stay by my side." So the night, and its memory, which cannot be separated, are impossibly precious. In retrospect, "the present" is just a memory in real time.

"We aren't gaolers," Proust's father says, if we take the

narrator to be a stand-in for Proust, but the child did feel like his bedroom was a cell, a place for time to be borne. In the winter of 1940, the Polish artist and writer Józef Czapski was in a Soviet prison camp, and he was thinking about Proust. He was among a small group of officers and soldiers who survived the internment; thousands of others were executed. In Czapski's words—he writes it, using the same phrase, twice—those others "disappeared without a trace." To occupy themselves, to keep their intellects sharp, to prove they were "still capable of thinking and reacting to matters of the mind," Czapski and his comrades in the camp delivered a series of lectures to one another. "Each of us spoke about what we remembered best," he writes, be it architectural history or mountain climbing. For Czapski, who had studied painting in France and been friendly with some of Proust's old friends, that subject was *In Search of Lost Time*. As the painter and translator Eric Karpeles writes in his introduction to *Lost Time: Lectures on Proust in a Soviet Prison Camp*, "A prisoner's constant state of vigilance was surprisingly conducive to the reclamation of memories." It came back to him there, in the freezing ruins of a bombed convent, the way Combray came back to "Proust" when he was dozing off or when he tasted the madeleine dipped in linden tea. He delivered the talks in French because he'd read the novel in French—much as they say you should study for a test at the same time of day you'll be taking the test; you should suck on a peppermint during both, so the taste brings the knowledge back. "What Czapski remembered best was the quintessential book of remembering," Karpeles writes.

In preparation for his lecture, Czapski made a series of

elaborate diagrams, like crib notes in tiny, neat print, drawn over with lines and circles in different shades of ink. Several are reproduced in the volume, and these too are translated, meticulously re-created in color by Karpeles. On one spread of the insert, we see Czapski's notes on the right, partially in Polish, partially in French. In the middle of the page is a yellow oval with lines around it, a crude sun. Inside, in all caps, underlined in red: "A MORT INDIFFE-RENTE." In Karpeles's version on the left, the same yellow sun, the same thick red line: "INDIFFERENT DEATH." Some pale script to the lower right of Czapski's sun circle is almost unintelligible to me; in the translation, it looks like this:

> x PRECIOUS WOUND
> x A BIT MIRED IN
> THE FLESH

These strange visual poems, "a hybrid of writing and drawing" as Karpeles describes them, were meant to serve as an aide-mémoire. The cheat sheets were all Czapski had because, of course, he could not check his quotes, could not fact-check any of his notes. This makes the errors more touching. Karpeles notes a couple: Czapski replaces the word "madeleine," the most iconic detail of the novel and one of the most iconic in all modern literature, with the word "brioche." He calls an unnamed character Jeanne. "He has not misremembered her name," Karpeles writes, "he has simply provided her with one, which Proust had failed to do." I found a mistake too. Czapski speaks of finding Proust to be "almost Pascalian," then refers to a night in

Blaise Pascal's life "that will always remain known as Pascal's mystery,"

> a night yielding an intense vision of a super-terrestrial
> world which caused him forever after, until his death,
> to wear around his neck a small scrap of paper on which
> was inscribed these few words: "Tears, tears of joy."

I was reminded of Percy Shelley's corpse washing up onshore with a volume of Keats at his breast. Wanting to know more about this story, I googled the phrase "Pascal's mystery" and found nothing. Had Czapski confused Pascal's experience with the paschal mystery, or *le mystère pascal*—no relation? (It's from the Greek *pascha*, as in Easter, meaning "passing over.") It seems likely; he'd also gotten the inscription wrong. It was not just a few words but a longer prayer or poem, a transcription of his vision, which Pascal wrote out on a piece of parchment and sewed into the lining of his coat. Here's the passage in question:

> FIRE.
>
> GOD of Abraham, GOD of Isaac, GOD of Jacob
>   not of the philosophers and of the learned.
> Certitude. Certitude. Feeling. Joy. Peace.
> GOD of Jesus Christ.
> My God and your God.
> Your GOD will be my God.
> Forgetfulness of the world and of everything, except
>   GOD.
> He is only found by the ways taught in the Gospel.

Grandeur of the human soul.

Righteous Father, the world has not known you, but I
have known you.

Joy, joy, joy, tears of joy.

I've seen it rendered differently; sometimes "Fire" is underlined, sometimes it's "Fire!" But always, the "tears" line
is "Joy, joy, joy, tears of joy"—the word "joy" is repeated, not
"tears." Earlier, in his own footnote to the lecture, Czapski notes that he is quoting Goethe from memory, "perhaps distorting his text." He then quotes (or misquotes?)
the Russian writer Vasily Rozanov: "There's nothing easier than to quote a text precisely, you just have to check
the books. It's far more difficult to assimilate a quotation
to the point where it becomes yours and becomes part of
you." There's an intimate beauty in minor errors. "Pascal's
mystery," those "tears, tears of joy" around his neck, were
not Pascal's but Czapski's, a semi-invention, a collaborative
memory.

In a brief introduction to the lecture, written in 1944,
Czapski speaks of "the joy" of that time in the prison camp,
the "rose-colored light" of those hours spent giving and
listening to lectures, "where a world we had feared lost to
us forever was revived." Others in the camps were having
similar, peculiarly happy experiences, somehow between
or inside of their sufferings. The Polish writer Aleksander
Wat, while in Lubyanka, lucked into a Russian translation
of *Swann's Way* with a Marxist critical introduction. Reading Proust in Lubyanka, Wat writes in his memoir, *My Century*, was "one of the greatest experiences of my life . . . from
then on I had a completely new understanding, not only of

literature, but of everything." Czapski had only dabbled in Proust until bedridden with illness: "I only have typhoid fever to thank for rendering me so helpless over a whole summer that I was able to read his work in its entirety." I feel a small, perverse twinge of envy—not for the fever or torture or persecution, obviously, but for the life-altering encounter with a book that can happen in a season of despair.

I am always struck by depictions of happiness in wartime, in the darkest conditions—Chernobyl, concentration camps. In *Family Lexicon*, a memoir of life under fascism in Mussolini's Italy, Natalia Ginzburg writes: "Lola used to remember with great longing the time she spent in prison. 'When I was in jail,' she'd often say. She would recount how in jail she finally felt tremendously at ease, finally at home and at peace with herself." She considered it the "noblest time of her life." Ginzburg's father, during bombings, "wouldn't go down into the shelters . . . Under the roar and whistle of planes, he ran hugging the walls with his head down, happy to be in danger because danger was something he loved." When her father returns from a stint in prison, he seems "happy" to have been there. The people in her life treasure their worst experiences; the worst is the best. It's often said to be a form of resistance, to refuse to have pleasure taken away from you. But there's also something fundamentally life-affirming about proximity to death. We grow nostalgic for our pain, once it's safely in the past, because pain's intensity makes regular life look banal.

Part of Czapski's lecture concerns Proust's self-actualization as a writer. In this section he intentionally conflates Proust and the "hero" of the novel, which is probably what we'd now call autofiction, a novelization of the author's real life. On his way to a reception at the Hotel de Guermantes, Proust has "the sudden conviction of a book existing within him, with all its details, only waiting to be realized." He enters "a state of feverish clarity." As Czapski recounts it,

> He observes the assembled group of friends from his earlier life, already deformed by age, growing older, bloated or withering away, and then sees young people there emerging among them, a new generation who seem to harbor so poignantly the same hopes his old or dear friends once held. All this he sees with new eyes, lucidly, detached, and from a distance; finally, he knows what he is meant to do with his life.

The force of the realization is such that "death has become a matter of indifference to him." Czapski uses the phrase once more, at the end of the lecture, this time clearly in reference to Proust, the author, the living (or dying) man. He spent his last years mostly in bed, finishing and revising the novel of his life. Czapski writes: "It's not possible that he did not understand, given the state of his health, that the enormous and feverish effort required to keep on with his work would precipitate his end. But he had made up his mind, he would not take care of himself; death had become truly a matter of indifference to him."

"INDIFFERENT DEATH," as the diagram said. Around that yellow sun, there are echoing paradoxical phrases: "GRANDEUR + MISERY." "PRECIOUS WOUND." "DECADANCE OF FORMS OF JOY." "BLESSED SUFFERING." "HIS TRIUMPH HIS DEATH." A question,

encircled: "DEAD FOR GOOD?" And under "HIS TRI-
UMPH": "THEY WILL LIVE." Along with his comrades, Czapski found meaning and wonder in the prison
camp ("the hours spent with memories of Proust, Dela-
croix, Degas seemed to me the happiest of hours"), and they
survived. Czapski lived to the age of ninety-six. But he had
assimilated Proust's indifference to death, which is not the
same as an indifference to living. It's an apprehension of
existence so luminous that the threat of death recedes into
dim corners.

On Jealousy

Recently, reading a new book of poetry, I noticed a certain macabre playfulness, a signature of influence that reminded me of "Daddy." *Plath-y!*, I wrote in the margin beside the poem. I pulled my copy of Plath's *Collected Poems* off the shelf (inscribed *Merry Christmas, 1994, Mom & Dad*; I would have just turned fifteen) and reread "Daddy" for the whatever-eth time.

For much of my life I read "Daddy" quite literally, as a renunciation of Plath's father: "Daddy, daddy, you bastard, I'm through." She all but calls him Hitler, with his "neat mustache" and "Aryan eye." As Janet Malcolm points out in *The Silent Woman*, the poem "has had a mixed reception." She quotes Leon Wieseltier in *The New York Review of Books*, 1976: "Whatever her father did to her, it could not have been what the Germans did to the Jews." Irving Howe, writing in 1973, found "something monstrous, utterly disproportionate" in the metaphor. I think of the opening lines of Sharon Olds's poem "The Takers": "Hitler entered Paris the way my / sister entered my room at night." That reversal is astounding—*Hitler* takes after the *sister*. (My friend Chris, in grad school, read these lines and said simply, "No.")

However, in 2012, newly released FBI files on the

German-born Otto Plath suggested that he may in fact have been a Nazi sympathizer. As *The Guardian* reported at the time, "The files reveal that he was detained over suspected pro-German allegiance." Unlike her critics in the twentieth century, Sylvia may have had the inside scoop on those allegiances. She may have meant to literally call him a Nazi.

That doesn't close the case on "Daddy," though. His politics notwithstanding, there's little evidence that Sylvia harbored any hateful feelings toward her father. As noted in a short, rather wonderful article about Plath and her series of bee poems, which I found on the website of a Dublin beekeeping association: "His death when Sylvia was only eight years old deeply affected her feelings and thoughts for the rest of her life. Her mother writes that, when she was told of her father's death, she said: 'I'll never speak to God again!'" (Otto Plath was an entomologist and the author of an influential book called *Bumblebees and Their Ways*.)

Plath does not betray conscious resentment of her father in her journals; the opposite, in fact: "I rail and rage against the taking of my father, whom I have never known; even his mind, his heart; his face, as a boy of 17 I love terribly. I would have loved him; and he is gone." A few years later, she visits his grave: "I found the flat stone . . . right beside the path, where it would be walked over. Felt cheated. My temptation to dig him up. To prove he existed and really was dead." Her journals make it clear she harbored much more hostility toward her mother. In 1958 she wrote:

> I never knew the love of a father, the love of a steady blood-related man after the age of eight. My mother

killed the only man who'd love me steady through life . . . I hate her for that . . . I hate her because he wasn't loved by her . . . It was her fault. Damn her eyes.

It's misplaced blame—Otto died of diabetes—but evidently how she felt. So where did "Daddy" come from? What made her change her mind? I don't think she did—or not about him. She wrote the poem in 1962, shortly after she discovered her poet-husband was having an affair with the striking Assia Wevill, another writer and a mutual friend (I feel compelled to tell you that the beekeeping site misspells her name as Assia "Weevil"), and shortly before she, at last successfully, died by suicide. Given the timing, I now presume "Daddy" is mostly a veiled address to Ted Hughes: Hughes is the bastard she is through with.

I wrote a review of the book that had reminded me of Plath, and turned in my draft with a long digression containing much of the above material, trying but not expecting to get away with it. Sure enough, my editor suggested we cut it, because it "distracted a bit too spectacularly" from the book at hand. (What a brilliant bit of diplomacy.) I figured the rabbit hole I had fallen down was a sign that I should write about Plath at length. Time to remind the world how good her poetry is, I thought—no more of this focus on her persona, on her schoolgirl cuteness, on the mythology of her suicide. We tend to associate Plath with moody teenagers; we don't take her imagined readership seriously, so we take her less seriously as well.

Not long after this, I saw a link to a piece in *The New Yorker*, by its poetry critic Dan Chiasson, about Plath's last letters, which had just been published. I think I gasped out loud. It was coincidence, only, or else some manifestation of collective consciousness, but it meant that my new reobsession with Plath was not unusual; any old Plath fan would be thinking, and writing, about Plath again now. I felt cheated (like Plath at her father's grave, *I* had wanted to unearth her) and a little mad—mad that a critic, more famous than me, had gotten to her first!

The piece does the work I egomaniacally thought I might do—reestablishing her genius, in the context of her vulnerability, her tendency to be underestimated, her "façade of chipper enthusiasm." It quotes the five words of Plath's I'm most jealous of not having written: *I eat men like air.* (I once heard a theory that great lines of poetry are mostly one-syllable words; I see it all the time now.) The essay is compassionate and full of interesting detail—like who ended up with her fishing rod—and critical insight:

> Her mind was brilliantly off-kilter, its emphasis falling in surprising places. We hear less than we might like about major literary or historical events: a dinner with T. S. Eliot and Stephen Spender in London, or her Tuesday-afternoon classes at B.U. with Robert Lowell, or drinks afterward with Anne Sexton and George Starbuck at the Ritz bar in Back Bay. It was unlikely that she could use these occasions in poems, and so, I think, they settled very lightly on her consciousness. But a groundhog—that she knew she could use.

I was mad it was so good.

There's a double bind in the work of writing, a trap of specificity: If you don't write about things people are interested in, nobody is going to read you. But if you write about things people *are* interested in, other people are writing about them too. It's true of all my favorite subjects—the great writers have already written about them. What can I possibly add? Janet Malcolm covered Plath and Hughes, psychoanalysis, Gertrude Stein, and true crime. Susan Sontag seems to have already had all my worthwhile thoughts, the thoughts I thought were *mine*. Reading writers I admire writing about things I want to write about, obsessions I'm protective of, makes me feel less special—a childish thing to feel, or at least to admit.

Doesn't everyone want to be special, though? In an interview in 2015, the novelist and screenwriter Bruce Wagner, who writes a lot about fame, said the following:

> Of course Warhol said everyone will be famous for 15 minutes, but I think the new model of that mantra is that in the future—which is now—everyone will be famous all the time. I think fame has a really interesting place in our being human. The desire for acclaim is not new—the attention one calls to self. An old Buddhist text said that the desire for acclaim is so strong that in many ways it's a more difficult hardship to overcome than poverty or disease. This particular Buddhist text I was reading said that even the most reclusive of cave monks will have the desire to be known the world over as the most reclusive of cave monks.

That last part—"even the most reclusive of cave monks will have the desire to be known the world over as the most reclusive of cave monks"—remains one of the most comforting things I have ever read. Actually, "comforting" doesn't do it justice—it's an exhilarating idea. I recite it to myself like a mantra. Wanting to be special isn't special.

The novelist Javier Marías wrote a weekly column for the Spanish newspaper *El País* for over twenty years. In many of these pieces, collected in his book *Between Eternities*, he seems preoccupied with the idea of uniqueness, and at least as jealously possessive of his subjects as I am. In one piece, "The Isolated Writer," he describes the writer's "need to feel *almost* unique, rather than the mere interchangeable member of a generation or group." How awful, to appear to be the product of the arbitrary coordinates of your time and place of birth! Without the illusion that we can reach escape velocity and transcend our zeitgeist, we'd be unable to work; our books would seem "superfluous." The title is wishful, then. (In his novel *The Infatuations*, one character expounds on the "glee" in obituary writing: how headlines like "Death of the last great cinema legend" suggest we are "joyfully celebrating the fact that, finally, there are no more geniuses." Less competition.)

In another column, he writes of the irritation of finding that your favorite art or artists have other fans. After naively believing "we were the only people who knew them, or at least the ones who best or most truly understood them," we learn that many others have felt the same, and then we see them as "usurpers" or "copycats." I've had a slightly different worry, that once someone more famous than me has written about "my" subject, everyone will think that *I'm* the copycat. For Marías—who I guess doesn't have to worry about writers more famous than him—this having to share is worse when the others are "people we don't like, or whom we detest or despise, or who strike us as arrant fools." Again, my worry differs—the pain of sharing is more poignant when I like the writer, when I see the writer who got there first was at least as interesting on the topic as I might have been. So what need of me, what need for me?

Marías ends "The Isolated Writer" with a passage about winning the Austrian State Prize for European Literature, a distinction he shares with such people as W. H. Auden, Italo Calvino, and Simone de Beauvoir. "These were figures whom I viewed almost as extraterrestrial beings, some ever since I was a child, and who, I was sure, bore no resemblance to myself," he writes. One might think that such an accolade would finally make one feel truly special. But, for Marías, to see his name added to this list of literary greats is paradoxically diminishing: It "makes me somehow less myself," he writes. It "makes me exist less."

This is like achieving satori, an understanding of the principle of "no self," via fame. How counterintuitive. It suggests that the cave monks, in their yearning for renown, were doing something right.

The Intolerable, I Guess

Sylvia Plath wrote her first poem, two lines about Christmas titled "Thoughts," when she was five. She was just eight—it was the year after her father died—when her first published poem appeared in the *Boston Herald*. For Plath, success was a lifelong skill in itself, separate from writing. Such was her professionalism, her touch with editors, publishers, and committees, you could fairly say she discovered Ted Hughes and made him famous. She read his poetry before she met him, in the first and only issue of *Saint Botolph's Review*, a pamphlet he and his Cambridge friends started in 1956 to publish one another's work. She bought a copy for one shilling and sixpence from Hughes's friend Bert Wyatt-Brown. Soon she had pedaled her bike furiously back through the February fog to Wyatt-Brown's station outside a pub, demanding to be told if he knew Hughes and Luke Myers, whose poems had taken her head off, and who had made her feel her own poems were precious and slight, "smug and little."

Wyatt-Brown invited her to the magazine's launch party that night. It was the party where she got "very very beautifully drunk," as she wrote in her journals, and, as a way of making an impression, bit Hughes on the cheek hard enough to draw blood. At our historical remove, the match looks star-crossed, Shakespearean. She had resisted the pull of marriage or even commitment to previous long-term boyfriends—there were many; she was boy crazy, and approached dating with the vigor of a sport—in order to focus on her career. She knew domestication and children would steal time from her writing. But Hughes was the first man she respected as her intellectual equal or better. She was tall, and he was taller, an imposing, strong-chinned presence (Anne Sexton nicknamed him "Ted Huge"), so attractive he reportedly made women throw up. Within four months of the party they had married in a secretive ceremony—Plath was afraid to lose her Fulbright scholarship—and later that same year, when she heard about a first-book contest jointly sponsored by Harper and the New York Poetry Center, she entered Hughes's manuscript, *The Hawk in the Rain*, not her own. She had a feeling he would win, and he did.

In her comprehensive biography *Red Comet: The Short Life and Blazing Art of Sylvia Plath*, the scholar Heather Clark goes deep into Plath's closest relationships—with her mother, her psychiatrist, her mentors and benefactors, her long-term correspondents and on-and-off boyfriends— but deepest on her great tempestuous love with Hughes. The image on the cover is a photo of Plath gazing up into Hughes's eyes, with a look of admiration and conspiratorial understanding—but you'd have to be familiar with the photo to know, as Hughes is cropped out. Plath loved him with the voracious passion she had for life in general. "She wanted to *do* everything herself, you see," her midwife, Winifred Davies, said. "She wanted to ride. And she wanted a cow so she could learn to milk. And she wanted bees so she could keep bees." Plath's friend David Compton called her "an enormous enthusiast for everything." For everything! She worshipped the clean, sunny beaches of her native New England, but also loved the moors where Hughes grew up—the ideal exterior setting for interior drama. She also loved to eat, and after Plath and Hughes visited W. S. Merwin and his wife, Dido, at their farmhouse in France, Dido complained that Plath polished off for breakfast what she'd planned to serve for lunch. (Plath was pregnant with her second child at the time.)

There were two sides to Plath, Plath who was obsessed with doppelgängers and doubles. There was the joyful hedonist who took such sensual pleasure in living, in birds and in trees, theater and art. She loved "the thinginess of things," and treated books with talismanic importance. She also loved drinking and sex and called herself "a good tart" in a letter to Ruth Beuscher, the doctor she grew close to at McLean Hospital, where she received shock treatment following her suicide attempt in 1953. Her ambition was part of her hunger for existence—she once wrote in her journal, "My life, I feel, will not be lived until there are books and stories which relive it perpetually in time." This Plath, who saw publication as a form of afterlife, was determined and persistent. In 1959, she was on a road trip with Hughes in the American West (in Yellowstone, their car was attacked by a bear) when she learned via letter that Knopf had rejected her manuscript, an early version of *The Colossus*. Her mother, Aurelia, suggested she consider revision, but Sylvia refused, writing back: "PLEASE don't worry about my poetry book but send it off . . . I have gone over it very carefully and am not going to try to change it to fit some vague abstract criticism . . . You need to develop a little of our callousness and brazenness to be a proper sender-out of mss." She almost always, in her letters to Aurelia, emphasized happiness and put up a brave front, as though impervious to rejection.

But Plath also had a vulnerable, defeated side, laid bare in the privacy of her journals. When she lost the 1959 Yale Younger Poets prize to George Starbuck—her former drinking buddy, if the term can apply to martinis at the Ritz—she found the irony awful: the editor said her poems were too "rough," when she'd worked so hard to break herself of technical perfection, of "archaic cutie tricks" at the expense of emotional force. She had wanted her poems to be more like Hughes's. "Will I ever be liked for anything other than the wrong reasons?" she wrote in her diary; "I have no champions." Of course, she had many, throughout her life. She published poetry, fiction, and criticism regularly in high-profile publications such as *The Atlantic* and *The Observer*; she had a coveted first-refusal contract with *The New Yorker*. But defeat came and went like a mood: the tides of failure. For Plath, success often felt like a failure—like the wrong success, too commercial or obscure; success insignificant, compared with her husband's; success badly won; success too late.

It was arguably Plath's rejection from Frank O'Connor's fiction class at Harvard in 1953 that set off the depressive episode that almost killed her. She was on her way home from an exhausting summer internship at *Mademoiselle* in New York City (a summer lightly fictionalized in her only published novel, *The Bell Jar*) when she got the news. O'Connor later said he thought Plath too advanced for the beginner-level workshop, but she didn't know this. She was supposed to be working on her senior thesis, on *Ulysses*. But she was overcome with a malaise she couldn't think through, an inability to read. Esther Greenwood, her counterpart in *The Bell Jar*, has a parallel struggle with *Finnegans Wake*:

> I squinted at the page.
> The letters grew barbs and rams' horns. I watched them separate, each from the other, and jiggle up and down in a silly way. Then they associated themselves in fantastic, untranslatable shapes, like Arabic or Chinese.
> I decided to junk my thesis.

Plath too abandoned the paper on Joyce, eventually submitting a thesis on doubles in Dostoyevsky instead.

It was an interesting experience to read *Red Comet* during quarantine. Clark's publisher was not printing physical galleys, and I don't use an e-reader, so I had my advance PDF, a 1,152-page document, printed and bound in two unwieldy, eight-by-eleven-inch volumes. I couldn't comfortably read them in bed or on the couch; I read them sitting at our kitchen table, over many nights and weekends of the sad, unsummery summer. Like Esther in her fictional room, and like so many others in the year 2020, I had intermittent difficulty focusing. I'm not normally prone to headaches, but through much of the spring and summer, a tingling knot of pain was lodged at the back of my skull. I found a chart online about the twenty or so known varieties of headache; mine was almost certainly a tension headache, associated with stress and depression. It was, in a way, difficult to read about Plath during this time, especially when I reached the biography's third and final section; I had a panicky awareness of the clock ticking down, a despair that I couldn't save her. In another way, the struggle gave me purpose—for days, it's what I did with my free time; it was what I had to do—and it was oddly kind of comforting to read about someone who suffered more than me, during what had been, up till then, the most difficult, anxiety-ridden period of my life. There were times when I missed my mother so much I forgot she was still alive.

Red Comet is almost a week-by-week telling of Plath's life story. Chapter 2 contains a full page about Plath's first words and pseudowords: at eight months, her lexicon included "Mama, dad, bye-bye," and "tick-tick," and at fifteen months, she'd announce "ga-ga" if she wanted attention. In Chapter 3, we get a list of the ten Girl Scout badges she earned in May of 1944. Later, we learn the details of many a date night with many a minor character. In Chapter 8, we learn one Constantine took her to "a Russian bar on 14th Street" in New York, where they danced, she in a black velvet suit, and drank Moscow mules. This onslaught of information can make for tiresome reading, though the gossip is occasionally fun; Yoko Ono makes a brief appearance in Chapter 13. At times, the book feels more like a resource for fact-checkers, a guide to the abundant existing material on Plath, rather than a book you're meant to read from cover to cover. It doesn't help that Clark's prose can look a little lifeless compared with both Plath's and Hughes's, which she quotes from frequently. Both poets were given to hilarious overstatement. Plath complained in a letter of the couple upstairs: "They live like pigs . . . They are unbelievable & don't deserve to live." (Clark's comment is "Sylvia's nastiness was out of all proportion.") Their writing is full of vivacity and style. In a letter to his sister, Olwyn, about American bread, Hughes called it "de-crapularised, re-energised, multi-cramulated, bleached, double-bleached, rebrowned, unsan-forised, guaranteed no blaspheming." He closed, "There is no such thing as bread." To his brother, Gerald, he wrote, "The food, the general opulence, is frightening. My natural instinct is to practise little private filthinesses—I spit, pee on shrubbery, etc, and have a strong desire to sleep on the floor."

Red Comet does stake some new ground, though it's diffi-cult in a field that already includes over a dozen biographies in addition to Plath's own copious journals and letters. It incorporates certain recently discovered and previously un-published letters (including several to her psychiatrist) and other archival materials, such as a portion of a lost novel, which Clark stumbled upon misfiled in an archive. She also claims to be more interested in tracing Plath's "literary and intellectual development" than other biographers, who have pathologized the poet and fixated on the macabre. As a crit-ical biographer, Clark is rather too credulous, too reverent of Plath's early writing. For example, Clark calls a descrip-tion in a 1943 letter to her mother of a book Plath had just read "the earliest surviving example of Plath's literary criti-cism." (She was eleven.) If other biographers have treated Plath's suicide as inevitable, it seems equally misguided to read her grade-school verse as though her literary fame were inevitable. However, Clark's expository close readings of Plath's late poems can be striking and even thrilling. She boldly compares "Ariel" to Hughes's poem "The Thought-Fox," a likely influence on Plath: "But horses are larger, stronger, and faster than foxes; Plath's poem is the stronger of the two, the one with the more intensely rhythmic momentum, the more resounding final crescendo." (I agree—it's the Hughes poem that now looks slight.) She writes of the "uncanny impression" that "Edge," Plath's last poem, gives of "having been written posthumously." "The woman is perfected," the poem's first line reads—"not perfect, *perfected*," Clark notes, "like a work of art, an experiment, something controlled." The poem is "self-elegy," grafting "the world of de Chirico onto Yaddo's garden," "a poisoned arrow aimed at Hughes." Whatever new territory the book covers, Clark is at her best when trained on the parts of Plath's life that have already received the most attention: her two suicidal episodes, a decade apart, and the literally feverish period of productivity in late 1962 and early 1963, when she was afflicted with recurring bouts of flu and an infection that nearly cost her her thumb, and when she wrote the unforgettable poems that appear in *Ariel*, published after her death.

In a chapter titled "The Hanging Man," Clark recounts the circumstances surrounding Plath's incredible first attempt at suicide—incredible because she failed, or because she succeeded, depending on which side of Plath was in question, the side that wanted to die or the side that wanted to live. On August 24, 1953, she left a note for her family, claiming she had gone on a walk, then swallowed around forty sleeping pills. She passed out in a crawl space in the basement, which was hidden behind a pile of firewood. She was "missing" for two days. "An astonishing 253 newspaper articles published about Plath's disappearance that August appeared as far afield as Los Angeles, Chicago, New York, and Florida," Clark writes—"a media frenzy." It's remarkable that Plath was still alive on August 26, when the family and Plath's friend Pat O'Neil heard a dog howling outside the house and realized, "all of us at the same instant," in O'Neil's telling, "that the dog was trying to tell us something." It was Sylvia's brother, Warren, who found her behind the firewood. She had vomited up the pills, but kept banging her head on the ceiling of the crawl space and falling back into unconsciousness. She later claimed she'd been smashing her head that way on purpose, and in the hospital raged with "a hatred toward the people who would not let me die, but insisted rather in dragging me back into the hell of sordid and meaningless existence." The gash on her head was infected and crawling with maggots when they saved her. "They had to call and call," Plath writes in "Lady Lazarus," "And pick the worms off me like sticky pearls."

In January of 1954, Plath was released from the hospital. Warren was driving her back to college at Smith when the car spun out in a blizzard. After rising from the ashes of the crawl space, the thought of death now unwished for, out of her own control, seemed cruelly unfair, the act of "malicious gods." "This can't happen to us," she thought; "we're different." Different why? Because we are *we*, not them. Any person is the only self. There was much left to do and experience—Plath had once written, in a letter to her mother, about throwing on clothes in preparation for a last-minute blind date, "all the time ranting . . . how never to commit suicide because something unexpected always happens." Suddenly you're glad you didn't fold. A few years later she was traveling around Europe and building a life with Hughes, her "genius husband" and *âme sœur*, whom she felt she was designed for: "I love his good smell and his body that fits with mine as if they were made in the same body-shop to do just that."

Though Plath was in many ways unconventional for her time, she was not interested in an open marriage. When, in mid-1962, Hughes embarked on an affair with Assia Wevill, the shock of the betrayal, the dissolution of Plath's Eden, was too much to bear. It puts me in mind of the letters Elizabeth Hardwick wrote to Robert Lowell after he left her alone in New York with their thirteen-year-old daughter; he'd met a woman at a party in London and moved in with her "instantly, that night." (The woman was Caroline Blackwood—like Wevill, another writer.) Hardwick could not fathom this abandonment. "You are going, irrevocably, to an emotionally crippled life, chaos, withdrawal," she wrote in a scathing missive. "We are utterly miserable, unbelievably wounded. I do feel as I say again that this is like a death." Her turmoil only worsened when she found out Lowell was writing poems about the breakup of their marriage, many of them drawing from the language of her letters: "I have never tried to deny my grief and pain and my love for you. For me at least the amputation will probably always hurt, but I am resigned to that. The recent shocks have added something new. I don't know what to call it—the intolerable, I guess."

Mutual friends encouraged Plath to let the affair blow over; such dalliances were normal, they said. They didn't believe it was really the end of the marriage. But she could not forgive Hughes this profound rejection—he seemed monstrous to her now. "I feel I am mourning a dead man," she wrote to Olive Higgins Prouty, a wealthy novelist who had funded Plath's scholarship at Smith and sent her regular checks for years. Hughes was "the most wonderful person I knew, and it is some stranger who has taken his name." Their children, Frieda and Nicholas, were then a toddler and an infant. Hughes and Plath had always shared parenting duties so they both could write—acquaintances marveled that he willingly changed "nappies"—but abruptly the sacrifice, the burden of their care along with Plath's, seemed too much for Hughes. "I'm aghast when I see how incredibly I've confined & stunted my existence," he wrote in a letter to Olwyn. The affair was a kind of tantrum, the expression of a sudden desperate need for personal freedom, for escape.

One night, feeling "deserted" and "mad with this solitude," Plath looked through the papers in Hughes's study at Court Green, their home in Devon. He was in London at the time. There were "sheafs of passionate love poems" he'd written for Wevill, describing "their orgasms, her ivory body, her smell, her beauty," as she wrote in a letter to Dr. Beuscher. They must have been torture for Plath to read, but "many are fine poems," she admitted. Plath herself was waking at four a.m. to write in the dark till the children got up. In a letter to the poet Richard Murphy, she wrote, "It is like writing in a train tunnel, or God's intestine." Elsewhere she called that time the "still, blue, almost eternal hour before cockcrow, before the baby's cry, before the glassy music of the milkman." Later that winter, she wrote to her mother, "Ted never liked blue, & I am a really blue-period person now." Color had always been important to her. The first stanza of "Ariel": "Stasis in darkness. / Then the substance-less blue / Pour of tor and distances." Hughes, like everyone else who read them, found these "dawn poems" astonishing. "She's like a woman on fire," he told a friend at the time. "They're extraordinary. The best things she's ever done." They could speak hatefully of each other—she called him an "apocalyptic Santa Claus"; he spoke of her "particular death-ray quality"—but their respect for each other's work until the end, their far apart ends, I find heartbreaking.

Plath wasn't in her right mind. She knew she was writing "on the edge of madness." She had moved with the children into a flat on Fitzroy Road where W. B. Yeats, one of her favorite poets, had lived. She was cold all the time—it was a notoriously frigid, unusually snowy winter—overworked, undereating, and taking a dubious cocktail of medications including codeine and an early antidepressant (which, like many antidepressants, is initially associated with an increase in the risk of suicide). She was terrified of herself. On January 27, 1963, she showed up crying in her downstairs neighbor's apartment, telling him, "I don't want to die. There's so much I want to do." She still wanted more life, and the metalife of more writing. To Dr. Beuscher she wrote, "I am scared to death I shall just pull up the psychic shroud & give up." She was scared to death of death, of death by her own hand, as if by some Greek prophecy, which would cut her off from the life she so desired—but death might also offer a release from all that fear. If she did it, she could stop imagining it. Which side would prevail? She feared her resolve, what she perceived in her poems as her godlike power, a resolve that could serve or betray her—she knew, if she crawled into the "grave cave" of Lady Lazarus again, she might not be saved.

Some have speculated that Plath expected to be rescued, as she had been before. But "the information now available," Clark writes in her epilogue, suggests otherwise. Plath's doctor at the time, John Horder, believed her calculations too precise: "He was one of the first to arrive at Fitzroy Road that morning," Clark writes, "and he would never forget the care Sylvia had taken to seal off the kitchen." (Her method—Plath turned on the gas oven, made a pillow with a towel, and laid her head on the oven door—was common in that era.) Plath had told some friends and family that Hughes wanted her to kill herself, but this is not corroborated and is hard to believe. Much of the epilogue contends with Hughes's enduring guilt. (Clark's devotion is to Plath, but she doesn't demonize Hughes, like the fans who repeatedly scratch his last name off her gravestone.) "It doesn't fall to many men to murder a genius," he said to one friend. "I don't ever want to be forgiven." Time became dilated for him, warped: "Immediately after Sylvia's suicide, he 'felt it had happened a month ago.' A month later, he wrote the Merwins, he felt it had 'happened yesterday.'" There are some indications the couple were on the verge of a reconciliation, but Plath might have been too proud to allow this or hope for it. "I depended on a resilience in her that I was too blind to see wasn't there," Hughes wrote.

But perhaps the resilience was there—she'd just turned her resilience against life. In an essay in *Seduction and Betrayal*, published in 1974, Elizabeth Hardwick observes, "Committing suicide is desperation, demand for relief, but

I don't see how we can ignore the way in which it is edged with pleasure and triumph in Sylvia Plath's work." In "Lady Lazarus," she continues, suicide is "performance," "an assertion of power, of the strength—not the weakness—of the personality." Lady Lazarus—"I am your opus"—is no victim.

In her 1962 poem "Elm," Plath wrote: "I am terrified by this dark thing / That sleeps in me; / All day I feel its soft, feathery turnings, its malignancy." Thanatos was lurking like a predatory owl in the hole of a tree. Even at her weakest, Plath knew her strength, her attraction to control. She was right to be frightened.

Against Completism

When I heard that a previously unpublished short story by Sylvia Plath would appear as a stand-alone volume in January of 2019, I requested an electronic galley and then let the file sit unopened in my inbox for several weeks. I felt apprehensive, even frightened of it. I wanted to write about it, but what if I didn't like it? I read *The Bell Jar* so long ago, when I was fourteen or so, that I couldn't remember anything about it. But I read *The Catcher in the Rye* around the same age, and I remember that book clearly. Had I only meant to read *The Bell Jar*, and never finished it? *Oh God*, I thought, *what if none of Plath's fiction is good?*

I decided to read *The Bell Jar* again before addressing the short story. The first, striking sentence—always already subsumed with death—gave me hope: "It was a queer, sultry summer, the summer they electrocuted the Rosenbergs, and I didn't know what I was doing in New York." Isn't that good? Really good first sentences so often include a proper name—the *Moby-Dick* effect—and manage to be both specific and mysterious. By the end of the first paragraph, I was nervous again: "It had nothing to do with me, but I couldn't help wondering what it would be like, being burned alive all along your nerves." Then, a hard return and a single-sentence paragraph: "I thought it must be the worst thing in the world." Plath's journals and letters are often unintentionally funny in their absurd dramatics—in 1956, after lending some books to a friend who returned them with underlining in pencil, she wrote in her journal, "I was furious, feeling my children had been raped, or beaten, by an alien." (I threw back my head laughing, reading alone on my couch.) The silliness of calling being executed "the worst thing in the world," a kind of understatement by overstatement, is rendered sillier by giving it its own paragraph. *Oh God*, I thought, *Sylvia Plath doesn't understand how paragraphs work.*

Having read the whole novel, I can confirm that Sylvia Plath doesn't understand how paragraphs work. There are many regrettable moments—Plath was Waspy and of-her-time—and over and over she uses foreignness as a metaphor, to represent the exotic or dangerous or wrong. Esther Greenwood "collected men with interesting names." For "interesting," read not-American. When she loses her tan, she looks "yellow as a Chinaman." I hate to even type that—it reminds me of Mickey Rooney's horrifying yellow-face in *Breakfast at Tiffany's* (released the year before Plath turned in her manuscript). But if you can get past this, as I can (I forgive the past a lot; the present is terrible too), *The Bell Jar* is a justifiable classic, shimmering with insight and good jokes. It does that thing that poets' novels do—it moves unpredictably, with the kind of I'm-not-entirely-sure-what-I'm-doing quality that can make for excellent dancing. At one point, a brute of a man forces Esther to tango, despite her protests that she doesn't know how; he says, "You don't have to dance. I'll do the dancing . . . Pretend you are drowning." And though the book can feel naive and sheltered, it's *about* how women are sheltered, how their lives are so prescribed (or were, at least, in the fifties) that even making an active choice comes down to choosing between levels of passivity, between being dragged across the dance floor or remaining in your seat. (Later, the woman-hater throws Esther into the mud and tries to rape her. "It's happening," she thinks. "If I just lie here and do nothing it will happen.")

The Bell Jar is not just autobiographical, but metafictional, which may be the defining characteristic of the poet's novel. It's a category I've been thinking about since reading *Eleanor, or, The Rejection of the Progress of Love*, by the poet and translator Anna Moschovakis. *The Bell Jar*, like *Eleanor*, and like Ben Lerner's *10:04*, and Jordan Castro's *The Novelist*, is about someone writing a novel—a poet writing a novel. (Lerner's begins with a young writer celebrating his massive advance.) Moschovakis once claimed that she only likes novels that are aware they're made of language. A meta-novel necessarily calls attention to the fact that it's a written thing, constructed out of words, and not a rubric for something nonlinguistic, the way some novels feel like novelizations of the movies they hope to become. Poems too are always reminding you they're made of language—a line break that creates an ambiguity, a non sequitur, an eye rhyme that halts the way your brain tries to visualize the story, and makes you look at words as symbols again. It may be, too, that poets are self-conscious about their fiction, and they mask that self-consciousness by highlighting it, a sheet thrown over a ghost. *The Novelist* can be read as a parody of writerly ineptitude. The narrator is always overdetailing his actions: "I raised my left arm and opened the left side of the cupboard, then raised my right arm and opened the right side of the cupboard." He considers fixing his failed draft by changing the tense and point of view, the way a poet improves a poem by changing the font.

My favorite metamoment in *The Bell Jar* is in Chapter 10, when Esther sits in her mother's breezeway with a typewriter and endeavors to begin her novel: "From another, distanced mind, I saw myself sitting on the breezeway, surrounded by two white clapboard walls, a mock orange bush and a clump of birches and a box hedge, small as a doll in a doll's house." She creates a "heroine" ("My heroine would be myself, only in disguise"), names her Elaine, and makes of Elaine her own doll as Plath has done with Esther— nested dolls. "Elaine sat on the breezeway in an old yellow nightgown of her mother's waiting for something to happen," Esther types. She notes that "Elaine" has six letters, like "Esther"—and, of course, like "Sylvia," although Plath originally published the novel, due to its potentially hurtful nature, under the pseudonym Victoria Lucas. My other favorite moment is almost accidentally meta. Esther goes skiing with her annoying boyfriend, Buddy Willard, and she knows she's not ready to ski down the big slope yet, but Buddy insists. "It never occurred to me to say no." She hasn't learned how to "zigzag," so she aims "straight down." She, like her real-life doppelgänger did, is about to break her leg in two places: "I plummeted down past the zigzaggers, the students, the experts, through year after year of doubleness and smiles and compromise, into my own past." This so beautifully encapsulates Plath's whole life it stabs me in the heart.

By this point I was excited about the short story, "Mary Ventura and the Ninth Kingdom." And then my expectations were subverted again—it's disappointing. At the level of the action, there's not much going on: a girl gets on a train, she meets a woman, the woman is mysterious, the train is mysterious. Eventually we, and Mary, understand that it's a train toward death, if not literal then metaphorical: the bleak, nonchosen future. At the level of the prose, there's not much going on: a lot of flat descriptions, a lot of ROYGBIV: "She took the seat by the window, slipping out of her red coat first and hanging it on the brass hook next to the windowframe . . . A lady in a blue jacket, carrying a baby wrapped in a soiled white blanket, paused at Mary's seat for a minute, but then continued to the back of the car." Then comes another woman "lurching down the aisle," "an earth-colored brown satchel in her hand," "her blue eyes crinkled up in a mass of wrinkles." The two walk to the diner car and order ginger ale and coffee. The older woman warms her hands with "the cup of steaming brown liquid." They go back to their seats and the woman buys a bar of chocolate; Mary helps herself to "the flat brown candy." All these color words do create a fantastical atmosphere, like a children's story (Plath herself described the story as a "vague symbolic tale"), but it's boring and lifeless. It was written in 1952, ten years before *The Bell Jar*, while Plath was at Smith, and it reads like what it is: an unpublished story someone wrote in college.

It's curious to read her journals from the same period, in late fall and early winter of 1952. She exhibits the wild mood swings of the depressive. In one entry she describes a luscious meal in detail ("Swordfish and sour cream broiled . . .

Hollandaise and broccoli. Grape pie and ice cream, rich, warm. And port, sharp, sweet . . . Good scalding black coffee"); she loved food. She's so optimistic and impatient for the future that "a lifetime is not long enough." In the very next entry, she despairs: "If ever I have come close to wanting to commit suicide, it is now." In mid-November, she's writing images that reappear in "Mary Ventura":

> I had lost all perspective; I was wandering in a desperate purgatory (with a gray man in a gray boat in a gray river: an apathetic Charon drawing upon a passionless phlegmatic River Styx . . . and a petulant Christ child bawling on the train . . .). The orange sun was a flat pasted disc on an [*sic*] smoky, acrid sky. Hell was the Grand Central subway on Sunday morning.

The next paragraph begins, "Tomorrow I will finish my science, start my creative writing story." In that story, Mary Ventura, a name Plath borrowed from a real friend, rides a train to hell; outside the air is "thick and smoky" from forest fires: "The train had shot into the somber gray afternoon, and the bleak autumn fields stretched away on either side of the tracks beyond the cinder beds. In the sky hung a flat orange disc that was the sun." She's the same writer as in her journals, but the effect is totally different—distant now, self-consciously *written*.

I've always thought of some writers as "hot" and others as "cold," my classic example being Plath versus Sexton, Plath the controlled ice queen and Sexton the sexy, messy one. But it's only Plath's poetry that's chilly; her journals and letters are lusty and overabundant with feeling, with overabundance. (In a funny but mean review of her recently published volume of letters, Jeffrey Meyers describes the "awkward" size and binding of the "massive volume," just one of two, the second of which will appear "to stupefied readers next fall.") It's hard to square Plath's prose with her poetry, the way it's hard to square her image in photographs—the beaming, teacher's-pet cuteness—with her deep, resonant voice on those spellbinding BBC recordings, where she sounds absolutely merciless, a dark sorceress. But her icy poetry is still intense, still burns to the touch— "black and glittering," as she writes in "Burning the Letters," from *Ariel*; "My veins glow like trees." In comparison, "Mary Ventura" feels dull and lukewarm.

Over dinner the night I read the story, I told John regretfully that I hadn't liked it. He reminded me of *The Original of Laura*, the unfinished work that Nabokov wanted destroyed, but that his son published anyway. Dmitri Nabokov claimed that his father appeared to him as an apparition and told him, "with an ironic grin": "You're stuck in a right old mess—just go ahead and publish!" The "manuscript" was really a stack of 138 handwritten index cards, so they gave it the subtitle "A Novel in Fragments." Nobody liked it. In a review for *The Guardian*, Martin Amis wrote, "Writers lead a double life. And they die doubly, too. This is modern literature's dirty little secret. Writers die twice: once when the body dies, and once when the talent dies." In *The Wall Street Journal*, Alexander Theroux wrote, "It is a pity that [Nabokov's] instructions were ignored and the novel survived in such a form. English professors may assign *The Original of Laura* to their students someday, but it is really better suited to a college ethics class." One thinks of the much-hated *Go Set a Watchman*, too, an early draft of *To Kill a Mockingbird* that was published in 2015 as a sequel. I saw an article about a couple who had named their child Atticus and were considering changing it, although he was five or six.

I'm not sure how I feel about posthumous publishing, or posthumous desire. What should happen to our desires? How long do they live, where do they go? Whatever the ethics, I'm glad we have Kafka; most of Plath's work was published after her death. In the introduction to Plath's *Collected Poems*, Hughes notes that toward the end of her life, she was in the habit of saving and dating her drafts:

> I have resisted the temptation to reproduce the drafts of these last poems in variorum completeness. These drafts are arguably an important part of Sylvia Plath's complete works. Some of the handwritten pages are aswarm with startling, beautiful phrases and lines, crowding all over the place, many of them in no way less remarkable than the ones she eventually picked out to make her final poem. But printing them all would have made a huge volume.

We now have huge volumes of Plath's life output, both what was intended for publication and what was not. I don't mind that it exists, but I don't want to read it, not all of it. *The Unabridged Journals of Sylvia Plath* is over seven hundred pages, including a twenty-five-page index, an index that renders it useful, accessible. I can enter it anywhere and leave anytime, like the internet. I would never read it from cover to cover, but I love to dip into the index and scan for compelling entries, of which there are many. What did Plath think of tarot cards, tattooing, Elizabeth Taylor (which one, the writer or the actress?), Dylan Thomas, *To Catch a Thief* ("motion picture"), Leo Tolstoy, the Eiffel Tower, Harry Truman? Thanks to this index I can read everything she wrote in her journals about her father, about her mother, about Jane Baltzell, later Jane Baltzell Kopp—a classmate of Plath's when she was on a Fulbright at Cambridge. She's the one who wrote in Plath's books so enragingly, and she's "the blond one" at the fateful party where Plath gets "very very beautifully drunk" and meets Hughes and bites him on the cheek. I can read everything she wrote about the real Mary Ventura: "I knew I would never have a friend quite like her . . . I love Mary . . . Mary is me."

There are eight citations for Marianne Moore, but just one for Marilyn Monroe. I don't know what Plath thought of Moore yet. (In his review of the letters, Meyers writes that Plath went from "hero-worshipping" "almost every published author" in college, calling Auden "the perfect poet," to "trashing the competition" while at Cambridge, including "her hated and more successful rival" Adrienne Rich—I guess this is supposed to reflect badly on her, but it sounds like every poet I know). But I read the one entry on Monroe, who, in October of 1959, came to Plath "in a dream, as a kind of fairy godmother": "I spoke, almost in tears, of how much she and Arthur Miller meant to us, although they could, of course, not know us at all. She gave me an expert manicure . . . She invited me to visit her during the Christmas holidays, promising a new, flowering life." Monroe overdosed on barbiturates in August of 1962, while Plath was finishing *The Bell Jar*. That Plath felt connected to Marilyn Monroe—as I'm sure Monroe would have felt connected to Plath, if she'd had a chance to read her—has magic. This dream sparkles, like Pinocchio's blue fairy godmother, floating in through the window. I don't want to exhaust these discoveries—a protective gesture. I'm saving something of her for myself, but also from myself.

Second Selves

I.

Jill Price has remembered every day of her life since she was fourteen years old. "Starting on February 5, 1980, I remember everything," she said in an interview. "That was a Tuesday." She doesn't know what was so special about that Tuesday—seemingly nothing—but she knows it was a Tuesday. This is a common ability, or symptom, you might say, among people with the very rare condition of hyperthymesia—excessive remembering—also known as highly superior autobiographical memory, or HSAM. All of the sixty or so documented cases have a particular, visual way of organizing time in their minds so their recall for dates is near perfect. If you throw them any date from their conscious lifetimes (it has to be a day they lived through—hyperthymesiacs are not better than average at history), they can tell you what day of the week it was and any major events that took place in the world; they can also tell you what they did that day, and in some cases what they were wearing, what they ate, what the weather was like, or what was on TV. One woman with HSAM, Markie Pasternak, describes her memory of the calendar as something like a Candy Land board, a winding path of colored squares (June is green, August yellow); when she "zooms in" on a month, each week is like a seven-piece pie chart. Price sees individual years as circles, like clockfaces, with December at the top and June at the bottom, the months arranged around the circle counterclockwise. All these years are mapped out on a timeline that reads from right to left, starting at 1900 until 1970, when the timeline takes a right-angle turn straight down, like the negative part of the y-axis. Why 1970? Perhaps because Price was born in 1965, and age five or six is usually when our "childhood amnesia" wears off. Then we begin to remember our lives from our own perspective, as a more or less continuous experience that somehow *belongs* to us. Nobody knows why we have so few memories from our earliest years, whether it's because our brains don't yet have the capacity to store long-term memories, or whether it's because "our forgetting is in overdrive," as Price writes in her memoir, *The Woman Who Can't Forget*.

Price was the first known case of HSAM. In June of 2000, feeling "horribly alone" in her crowded mind, she did an online search for "memory." In a stroke of improbable luck, the first result was for a memory researcher, James McGaugh, who was based at the University of California, Irvine, an hour away from her home in Los Angeles. On June 8, she sent him an email describing her unusual memory, and asking for help: "Whenever I see a date flash on the television I automatically go back to that day and remember where I was and what I was doing. It is non-stop, uncontrollable, and totally exhausting." McGaugh responded almost immediately, wanting to meet her. Her first visit to his office was on Saturday, June 24. He tested her recall with a book called *The 20th Century Day by Day*, asking her what happened on a series of dates. The first date he gave her was November 5, 1979. She said it was a Monday, and that she didn't know of any significant events on that day, but that the previous day was the beginning of the Iran hostage crisis. McGaugh responded that it happened on the fifth, but she was "so adamant" he checked another source, and found that Price was right—the book was incorrect. The same thing happened when Diane Sawyer interviewed Price on *20/20*. Sawyer, with an almanac on her lap, asked Price when Princess Grace died. "September 14, 1982," Price responded. "That was the first day I started twelfth grade." Sawyer flipped the pages and corrected her: "September 10, 1982." Price says, defiantly, the book might not be right. There's a tense moment, and then a voice shouts from backstage: "The book is wrong."

McGaugh and his research team also asked Price to recollect events from her own life. One day, "with no warning," they asked her to write out what she did on every Easter since 1980. Within ten minutes, she had produced a list of entries, which they included in the paper they published about Price, or "AJ" as they called her in the case notes, in 2006. The entries look like this:

April 6, 1980	9th Grade, Easter vacation ends
April 19, 1981	10th Grade, new boyfriend, H
April 11, 1982	11th Grade, grandparents visiting for Passover
April 3, 1983	12th Grade, just had second nose reconstruction

It continues through 2003. The team was amazed, in part because the date Easter Sunday falls on, in any given year, varies so much, and in part because Price is Jewish. McGaugh's team was able to verify the content of the entries because Price has kept detailed journals since 1976. She's protective of the journals; she doesn't like anyone to read them and she doesn't like to read them herself. But she showed them to the researchers, and she showed them to Barnaby Peel, the director of a 2012 documentary about hyperthymesia. The journal has "everything, everything, everything, everybody, everything," she tells Peel. It's written in tiny print on calendar-grid pages held together with paper clips. "I don't like lined paper," she says—it feels too constricting. He asks her how often she rereads it, and she says, "I don't reread any of it . . . I don't need to, I don't want to." She's defensive on this point because in 2009, the professor and science writer Gary Marcus wrote an article about her in *Wired* that she hated. In it he claimed that her incredible memory was really a form of obsessive-compulsive disorder, and the object of obsession her own life: "Why is her memory of her own history so extraordinary? The answer has nothing to do with memory and everything to do with personality. Price remembers so much about herself because she thinks about herself—and her past—almost constantly." He noted that "one simple method" of improving one's memory is keeping a journal. The implication, for Price, was that she was using her journals as a crib sheet, a study aid to memorize her days. "I don't write this to remember," she says to Peel. "I write it so I don't go crazy."

Hyperthymesiacs are prone to this kind of externalization, keeping some kind of ship's log to document their memories. Aurelien Hayman, a Welsh student who was twenty at the time he was featured in Peel's documentary, covered the walls of his bedroom with snapshots. Hayman thinks of photos as "the closest you can get to making a memory an object." A picture is "a concrete memory"—a kind of verification that persists into the present and exists outside the head. Hayman's memories, like those of others with HSAM, are already highly visual, an automatic memory palace. "It's like I could get a diary for 2009 and write it if I wanted to, retrospectively," he says—he can see the "imaginary pen writing in events in this sort of mental calendar." Bob Petrella, a stand-up comedian and TV producer, has a scrapbook-like album he calls by the recursive acronym B.O.B., the Book of Bob. He didn't write it in real time, like a diary, but re-created it from memory in 1999. It includes highlights from his life and a ranking of years from best to worst; his favorite year was 1983, then 1985 and 2004 are tied. Petrella clearly takes joy in the book and in his memories, unlike Price, who, by the time she was in her thirties, when she wrote to McGaugh, was deeply depressed and overwhelmed by her memories—by their volume, their hyperspecificity, their irrepressible immersiveness. Everyone has cues that will trigger certain memories, but for Price the cues are constant and the memories inescapable. "It's as though I have all of my prior selves still inside me," she writes in her memoir. If anything reminds her of a bad day, essentially she has to live the day again. She feels she is *in* those moments—living both the past and present, like a "split screen"—and the pain still hurts. She often falls into a pattern that she calls "Y diagramming," going back over her choices and all of their consequences: "If I hadn't done this, then that wouldn't have happened . . . It has instilled in me an acute, persistent regret." It's the line of causation that haunts her—she can see all the causes going back for forty years so clearly. Hyperthymesiacs can seem to get lost in the past; the remembering takes so much *time*. (Borges's "Funes the Memorious" is a fictional hyperthymesiac: "He could reconstruct all his dreams, all his half-dreams. Two or three times he had reconstructed a whole day; he never hesitated, but each reconstruction had required a whole day.")

There have been periods when Price stopped journaling for a while, but eventually "the swirl" in her head, the cascade of days, would get out of control and she would realize she "had to go back and get all of that time down." She'd then reconstruct the missing time day by day after the fact—she remembered the details whether or not she had written them down. It happens, the remembering, with no conscious effort. The journal is "a physical and emotional reassurance that the event really happened," she writes. "I can't accept living with just the memory. It has to be tangible—something I can hold on to physically, something I can handle." By "handle," I think she means both that she can touch it and that, because she can touch it, she can process and accept it; she can cope with the overpowering *reality* of reality. Most of us can cope with it, insofar as we can cope with it, because the reality passes so quickly and then begins to fade. (I think of Rilke, the end of "Portrait of My Father as a Young Man": "Oh quickly disappearing photograph / in my more slowly disappearing hand.") McGaugh's team believes that Price's condition is not an ability, a skill one could develop like the people who memorize digits of pi or the order of cards in a deck, so much as a disability. Her brain is very bad at forgetting—Price claims she has never misplaced anything, never once lost her wallet or her keys—but forgetting helps us live. Life, experienced once, in its excruciating fullness, is enough. As Ernest Becker writes in *The Denial of Death*, "full humanness means full fear and trembling." "Life itself is the insurmountable problem."

In her memoir, Price writes about "the memory bump," the spike in autobiographical memories that most people have between the ages of ten and thirty, a time that includes lots of novel experiences and during which people are actively forming their sense of themselves. She cites a study described in *Psychology Today*: "If you ask college students to tell you their most important memories, and then surprise them six months later by asking again, they will repeat stories at a rate of just 12 percent . . . Even when asked specifically, 'What is your first memory?' subjects will rarely mention the same one twice." So even though we have more memories during this period, or perhaps because we have more memories, the importance we assign to our memories is in flux. Our personalities, our *selves*, are likewise in flux; we choose the memories that serve our going narrative at the time. These narratives seem to be culture-bound—that is, they follow templates we absorb from the culture. Americans, according to the psychologist Dan McAdams, are drawn to redemption narratives, which frame the star as a hero, and their counterpart—the "contamination narrative," the idea that a certain event ruined everything afterward. Price thinks her memory changed irrevocably when she was eight years old and her father moved the family from New York City, where she'd had an idyllically happy childhood, to California for a job. But her highly specific memory didn't really feel excessive, didn't come to be a burden, until her twenties, when her life went unstable. Her mother almost died during surgery; her grandparents fell ill and died; her parents started fighting and eventually separated. So much change and strife, recalled in all its particulars, was too much for Price. She did not have the luxury of "choosing" to forget what she couldn't accept.

There's something strange about HSAM I never see mentioned. Price's father was an entertainment agent—he worked for the man who discovered Jim Henson, and she used to go with him to tapings of *The Ed Sullivan Show*, before they moved to California. Her mother was a dancer in a troupe that appeared on Broadway and TV in the 1940s and '50s. Price's first job was in TV, and she says she's "a TV fanatic." (In addition to her journals, she collects all kinds of objects and data from her life, and indexes the data: "In 1982 I started to make tapes of songs off the radio that I labeled meticulously by season and year, and I kept that up until 2003. I still have all of those tapes. In late 1988, I started making videos of TV shows, and I have a collection of close to a thousand of them. I also started an entertainment log in August 1989 in which I wrote down the name of every record, tape, CD, video, DVD, and 45 that I own." If memory is an index, Price also has an index to the index.) When Barnaby Peel quizzes Aurelien Hayman about what happened on June 17, 2008, one of the things he mentions (after clicking his tongue while thinking, a sound like a Rolodex, or the numbers turning over on an old-fashioned flip clock) is that Joan Rivers was thrown off a talk show for swearing. He can call up the dates that specific episodes of *Big Brother* aired—but bristles at any suggestion it means he's "obsessed" with the show. He says it means nothing to him. Bob Petrella worked in TV. The actress Marilu Henner is another of the few known people with HSAM. She describes her memory of a year as something like "selected scenes on a DVD." "It's like time travel," she says on a CBS clip. "I'm back looking through my eyes." In a *60 Minutes* segment from 2010, an interviewer asks her about a random episode of *Taxi* filmed more than thirty years earlier, in 1978. (The show ran for five seasons, 114 episodes.) She instantly remembers the dress she was wearing and one of Tony Danza's lines.

Why are so many of the well-known examples of hyperthymesia involved somehow with TV? Is it because TV helped them discover one another? That people who watch a lot of TV were more likely to hear about Jill Price and Marilu Henner and realize they weren't alone? I thought so at first, but now I wonder if it's actually a post-TV condition, a disease of modernity, if it is a disease. (Henner is a happy person—maybe it helps that she's rich and famous—but most people with hyperthymesia have difficult lives. For Alexandra Wolff, it feels as if "there are no fresh days, no clean slates without association." Another person with HSAM, Bill Brown, told an NPR reporter that he'd been in touch with most of the known cases, and that all of them had struggled with depression and very few—only two—had maintained a long marriage.) In his book *The Week: A History of the Unnatural Rhythms That Made Us Who We Are*, the historian David M. Henkin discusses the invention of the week. Unlike years (defined as the time it takes the earth to revolve around the sun) and months (which are based on the cycles of the moon), weeks are wholly man-made. The seven-day week has been around for centuries, but according to Henkin, television schedules helped solidify weeks as the stranglehold unit of our lives: "Saturday afternoon movies, weekly sitcom serials, and colossal cultural institutions such as *Monday Night Football* played a far greater role in structuring the American week than Wednesday theater matinees a century earlier, because they reached so many more people and faced so little competition." Maybe TV, as trains had before it, fundamentally altered how we think about time.

Jill Price has said that when she dies, she wants her journals, those external memories, to be buried with her body or "blown up in the desert," a literally Kafkaesque request. It's a refusal of the hope of "life" after death. If someone else could read her journals, Price's days might be lived through yet again—a prospect she must find gruesome and also unnecessary. (Reportedly Freud once said, after fainting, "How sweet it must be to die.") A journal is an effigy of the self, or else *is* the self, the self that exists because we create it. I am no longer sure, for the record, what people mean when they say that the self is illusory. Isn't it here? Here where I sit, and in what I am writing? Isn't it just my singular memory? Price understands this. The self dies with the self.

II.

I'm interested in the journals of writers (I suppose anyone who writes journals is a writer) as sites of self-loathing, of disappointment and failure. In his preface to *A Writer's Diary*, the volume of extracts from Virginia Woolf's diaries he edited, Leonard Woolf remarks that, even taken in full, "diaries give a distorted or one-sided portrait," because "one gets into the habit of recording one particular kind of mood—irritation or misery, say—and of not writing one's diary when one is feeling the opposite." Max Brod writes something similar in his postscript to Kafka's diaries, which he published against his friend's wish that they be "burned unread": "One must in general take into consideration the false impression that every diary unintentionally makes. When you keep a diary, you usually put down only what is oppressive or irritating. By being put down on paper painful impressions are got rid of." We can use them as a kind of confession booth, a place to expurgate our worst thoughts—so we don't "go crazy." Susan Sontag's son, David Rieff, in his preface to *Reborn: Journals & Notebooks, 1947–1963*, identifies the two primary moods of the notebooks as "pain and ambition." He writes of wanting to argue with her as he read them, to shout, "Don't do it," the way Sontag had seen the audience at a performance in Greece shout out at Medea. These editors were close to the authors, and must have felt their own impressions of the authors as people were more correct, more complete, than the version preserved in the diaries. But I'm not sure it follows. Aren't the grim, unflattering things you only share with your diary in a way your truer self? The self you are alone, in what Sontag calls "the ecstasy of aloneness"? Yet, she also writes, "I know I'm not myself with people . . . But am I myself alone? That seems unlikely too." If there is no *one* self, you can never *be* yourself, only one of your selves.

Sontag was prone to making lists of resolutions, lists of qualities she hated, lists of books to read and reread and art and films to see—lists as a method of betterment. The very first entry in her notebook from 1947 is a list of beliefs, which begins like so:

> I believe:
> (a) That there is no personal god or life after death
> (b) That the most desirable thing in the world is freedom to be true to oneself, i.e. Honesty
> (c) That the only difference between human beings is intelligence

She was fourteen years old—and already conceived of writing as commitment to belief. In 1948 she writes: "It is useless for me to record only the satisfying parts of my existence—(There are too few of them anyway!) Let me note all the sickening waste of today, that I shall not be easy with myself and compromise my tomorrows." This is writing as a way of making truth more true, if not creating truth out of nothing. Her notebooks, she writes, coincide with her "real awakening to life": "This has been a necessity for me for the last four years: to document + structure my experiences . . . to be fully conscious at every moment which means feeling the past to be as real as the present." The journals are a sort of supermemory, a more reliable and permanent record of experience, and of consciousness itself, which can't quite be captured outside writing, with a photo album, say—one could only guess at the moods and arrangements behind the pictures. Some writers keep a notebook as a sidecar, a paratext, while writing another book, to capture ideas and excess material and feelings about the process. A diary, then, is the footnotes to the project of our lives, to the self as a project.

Ten years later, in 1957, she writes this (unconscious?) revision to her list:

> What do I believe?
> In the private life
> In holding up culture
> In music, Shakespeare, old buildings

She adds, this time, a list of things she enjoys (music, again; being in love; sleeping) and a list of her faults:

> Never on time
> Lying, talking too much
> Laziness
> No volition for refusal

This distaste for talking, her own speech, comes up again and again: "The leakage of talk. My mind is dribbling out through my mouth." "I am sick of having opinions, I am sick of talking." "Important to become less interesting. To talk less, repeat more, save thinking for writing." Conversation *competes* with writing. In 1954 and 1955, the middle years of her marriage to Philip Rieff, the entries are scant. "Speech is so much easier + more copious compared to the labor of keeping a journal," she notes. She's not writing much because she's not alone—there is somewhere else for the language to go. (I remember, during the early pandemic, when we saw fewer people, I felt overburdened by language; all these things I *would* say, they were trapped in my mind. And writing them down made me feel less lonely, even if I didn't think anyone would read what I'd written.)

But she doesn't value what's easy, and would rather put the language into writing. "From now on I'm going to write every bloody thing that comes into my head . . . I don't care if it's lousy. The only way to learn how to write is to write." In 1957, when she separates from Rieff, the notebooks fill up again—there's no one else to observe her. Being self-conscious, she writes, is "treating one's self as an other." (That's one of those thoughts I had thought of as mine.) In an entry labeled "On Keeping a Journal," she writes, "I do not just express myself more openly than I could do to any person; I create myself. The journal is a vehicle for my sense of selfhood . . . It does not simply record my actual, daily life but rather—in many cases—offers an alternative to it." The journal forms a parallel universe, a better reality. I am struck by Sontag's ambition not just for fame and success but for real moral excellence. She wants to be a person who deserves success. She really wants to change.

In 1960, she writes a number of entries on a trait she calls "X," or "X-iness," the need to be liked, to please and impress other people, which she sees as very American, and which encourages her "tendency to be indiscreet," to gossip and name-drop ("How many times have I told people that Pearl Kazin was a major girlfriend of Dylan Thomas? That Norman Mailer has orgies?"). X is why she's a "habitual liar"—"lies are what I think the other person wants to hear." "All the things I despise in myself are X: being a moral coward . . . being phony, being passive." "People who have pride don't awaken the X in us," she writes; pride is "the secret weapon," the "X-cide." She hasn't solved this problem in herself by 1961; she's still telling herself "to smile less, talk less" . . . "not to make fun of people, be catty." "Don't smile so much, sit up straight, bathe every day, and above all Don't Say It, all those sentences that come ready-to-say on the tickertape at the back of my tongue." It's hard to imagine, despite all this evidence, that Sontag was ever a suck-up or a people pleaser, someone who smiles too much or too ingratiatingly. I have watched many times, though it makes me squirm, a clip of her speaking to Christopher Lydon, in 1992, with utter and withering contempt. Her only smiles are pitying. She dismisses all his questions as unserious. We can see she's achieved it, fame of course but also pride, the vanquishing of X.

Gide also made lists in his journals, lists of commitments and theories of living ("One ought never to buy anything except with love" . . . "*Take upon oneself as much humanity as possible*. There is the correct formula") and "rules of conduct." From an entry in 1890:

> Pay no attention to *appearing. Being* is alone important.
> And do not long, through vanity, for a too hasty manifestation of one's essence.
> Whence: do not seek to *be* through the vain desire to *appear*; but rather because it is *fitting* to be so.

He frequently chided himself: "I must stop puffing up my pride (in this notebook) just for the sake of doing as Stendhal did." When Sontag read Gide's journals, she identified so deeply with his thinking, she wrote, "I am not only reading this book, but creating it myself": "Gide and I have attained such perfect intellectual communion . . . Thus I do not think: 'How marvelously lucid this is!'—but: 'Stop! I cannot think this fast!'" Delightfully, Woolf felt the same, reading his journals in 1934: "Full of startling recollection—things I could have said myself." (When I mentioned this coincidence to John, he looked at me wide-eyed—"That's how *I've* always felt.") "Recollection" is an odd word, here—did she mean recognition? It suggests she *remembers* Gide's thoughts, experiences Gide's thoughts as memories, the way she does when rereading her own writing. ("To freshen my memory of the war, I read some old diaries.")

Woolf, like Sontag, would periodically go through and annotate her old journals after the fact, adding comments and asides and corrections of a sort. In late October of 1931, she notes the updated sales figures for *The Waves* ("It has sold about 6,500 today . . . but will stop now, I suppose") in the margin of an entry dated January 26, 1930, where she'd guessed "[it] won't sell more than 2,000 copies." To an entry about Arnold Bennett she adds: "Soon after this A.B. went to France, drank a glass of water and died of typhoid." In an entry dated April 27, 1925, Woolf notes that *The Common Reader* has been out five days and "so far I have not heard a word about it, private or public; it is as if one tossed a stone into a pond and the waters closed without a ripple." But she claims she is "perfectly content" with this silence, she cares less than she has ever cared. (I love Woolf's continual insistence that she's indifferent to her fame and her work's reception. In response to a "sneering review" two months later, she assures herself, "So from this I prognosticate a good deal of criticism on the ground that I'm obscure and odd; and some enthusiasm; and a slow sale, and an increased reputation. Oh yes, my reputation increases." Once she knew she had fame she found it "vulgar and a nuisance." I love the vanity of writers, and of famous dead writers especially.) In that same April entry, she digresses: "My present reflection is that people have any number of states of consciousness: and I should like to investigate the party consciousness, the frock consciousness etc." In the margin, she has added, at some point, "Second selves is what I mean."

Who is Woolf lying to, if she is lying, in these diaries? Herself, a little bit, the second self that is the diary, and the future Virginia, who might as well be another person entirely. In 1919, she writes, "I am trying to tell whichever self it is that reads this hereafter that I can write very much better." Later that year: "What a bore I'm becoming! Yes, even old Virginia will skip a good deal of this." At the age of thirty-eight, she writes:

> In spite of some tremors I think I shall go on with this diary for the present. I sometimes think that I have worked through the layer of style which suited it— suited the comfortable bright hour after tea; and the thing I've reached now is less pliable. Never mind; I fancy old Virginia, putting on her spectacles to read of March 1920 will decidedly wish me to continue. Greetings! my dear ghost; and take heed that I don't think 50 a very great age.

It seems we can't help but imagine an audience when we write. Because a journal makes the self external, the self counts as an audience. But I also think Woolf and Sontag, in saving their journals, just must have imagined that others might read them as well. They must have, because they loved reading writers' diaries. Sontag read Kafka's diaries. Kafka read Goethe's: "Distance already holds this life firm in tranquillity, these diaries set fire to it. The clarity of all the events makes it mysterious." (The next day he writes, "How do I excuse yesterday's remark about Goethe [which is almost as untrue as the feeling it describes, for the true feeling was driven away by my sister]? In no way." For Kafka, contra Sontag, writing the thing often made it *less* true, reduced the verity of pure thought to lies. "Nothing in the world is further removed from an experience . . . than its description." The words spoil reality.) Plath read Woolf's: "Just now I pick up the blessed diary of Virginia Woolf which I bought with a battery of her novels saturday with Ted. And she works off her depression over rejections from Harper's (no less!—and I hardly can believe that the big ones get rejected, too!) by cleaning out the kitchen. And cooks haddock and sausage. Bless her. I feel my life linked to her somehow." So did Eudora Welty, who quotes, or rather misquotes, from Woolf's diary in her *Paris Review* interview: "Any day you open it to will be tragic, and yet all the marvelous things she says about her work, about working, leave you filled with joy that's stronger than your misery for her. Remember— 'I'm not very far along, but I think I have my statues against the sky'? Isn't that beautiful?" Woolf's exact quote is: "It is bound to be very imperfect. But I think it possible that I have got my statues against the sky." (This makes me think of Czapski: "There's nothing easier than to quote a text precisely . . . It's far more difficult to assimilate a quotation to the point where it becomes yours and becomes part of you.")

A journal—any writing—is a chance at immortality, or

if not eternal life, at least a little more life, a little more after death. Rieff notes that his mother died "without leaving any instructions as to what to do with either her papers or her uncollected or unfinished writing." It makes sense because she didn't really believe she would die, as he describes in his own memoir of Sontag's terminal cancer. He contrasts her death to Simone de Beauvoir's mother's death, which she called "a very easy death"—with no internet, and differing medical ethics at the time, Beauvoir's mother died in ignorance of the severity of her illness. Sontag had no such luck, and though she knew intellectually how slim her odds of survival were, she couldn't help but hold out hope, even inside or beside her despair, and continued to make lists and notes and plans for travel and projects, "fighting to the end for another shard of the future." She was willing "to undergo any amount of suffering," according to Rieff, for a chance at more life, this despite her depression: she "wanted to live, unhappy, for as long as she possibly could." Woolf, although she killed herself, seemed also to believe she might not die—in 1926, she writes, "But what is to become of all these diaries, I asked myself yesterday. If I died, what would Leo make of them?" If! Ernest Becker would say no one really does or can believe it: "Our organism is ready to fill the world all alone . . . This narcissism is what keeps men marching into point-blank fire in wars: at heart one doesn't feel that *he* will die, he only feels sorry for the man next to him."

Woolf wanted her diary "to be so elastic that it will embrace anything"—as she had said the previous year of Byron's *Don Juan*, that the poem had an elastic shape that could hold any thought that came into his head, or as she said of the new form of novel she'd begun in 1920, which became *Mrs. Dalloway*, a form with "looseness and lightness" that could "enclose everything, everything." Like Jill Price's journals, the journals holding "everything, everything, everything, everybody, everything." A comprehensive diary exposes the near infinity of detail in a life, even a life as short as Plath's—the index to Plath's unabridged journals is almost thirty pages long and contains entries for apartheid, Louis Armstrong, the Aztecs, Brigitte Bardot, bees, Sid Caesar, Alexander Calder, *Un Chien Andalou*, circumcision, Marie Curie, demonic possession, the Detroit Tigers, Amelia Earhart, the Eiffel Tower, Paul Gauguin, Adolf Hitler, need I go on? Perhaps a life actually is infinite, like the points between zero and one on a number line. You could always make the journal longer, write in a finer degree of detail, add in more sense and observation, that is, if you had the time.

Woolf also wanted her published books to be more like the diaries. "Suppose one can keep the quality of a sketch in a finished and composed work? That is my endeavor." This is part of the beauty of journals—they remain forever sketchy, with the un-worked-over magic of first drafts. "It strikes me that in this book I practise writing; do my scales." This in 1924: "And old V. of 1940 will see something in it too. She will be a woman who can see, old V., everything— more than I can, I think." Here is a bit of the tragedy Welty referred to. By 1940 life was very difficult for Woolf, and not only because of the war, though the war is heavy too, inescapable as atmosphere: "One ceases to think about it— that's all. Goes on discussing the new room, new chair, new books. What else can a gnat on a blade of grass do?" Her friends' deaths have been hard: "There seems to be some sort of reproach to me . . . I go on; and they cease. Why?" "It's life lessened"—less life overall; their deaths seem to sap life from her. After Roger Fry's funeral, she writes: "A fear then came to me, of death. Of course I shall lie there too before that gate and slide in; and it frightened me." (How like Berryman's lines: "Suddenly, unlike Bach, // & horribly, unlike Bach, it occurred to me / that *one* night, instead of warm pajamas, / I'd take off all my clothes / & cross the damp cold lawn & down the bluff / into the terrible water & walk forever / under it out toward the island.") Seeing more, knowing more, having more to remember—it all has a cost, a weight.

Toward the end of her life, Woolf seemed to begin to view death as release from the fear of death. She writes more and more of death. On Sunday, June 9, 1940: "I don't want to go to bed at midday: this refers to the garage." ("The garage" is where Leonard had stashed away petrol, for use in the case that Hitler should win.) "It struck me that one curious feeling is, that the writing 'I' has vanished. No audience. No echo. That's part of one's death . . . this disparition of an echo." On June 22: "If this is my last lap, oughtn't I to read Shakespeare? But I can't . . . Oughtn't I to finish something by way of an end?" The war, she feels, "has taken away the outer wall of security"; "no echo comes back"; "I mean, there is no 'autumn,' no winter. We pour to the edge of a precipice . . . and then? I can't conceive that there will be a 27th June 1941." (There wasn't, for her.) On July 24: "I make these notes, but am tired of notes, tired of Gide." On September 16: "Mabel [the cook] stumped off . . . 'I hope we shall meet again,' I said. She said 'Oh no doubt' thinking I referred to death." On October 2: "Why try again to make the familiar catalogue, from which something escapes. Should I think of death?" She tries to imagine "how one's killed by a bomb":

> I've got it fairly vivid—the sensation: but can't see anything but suffocating nonentity following after . . . It—I mean death; no, the scrunching and scrambling, the crushing of my bone shade in on my very active eye and brain: the process of putting out the light—painful? Yes. Terrifying. I suppose so. Then a swoon; a drain; two or three gulps attempting consciousness—and then dot dot dot.

In her very last entry, written on March 8, 1941, she seems almost happy. She's been to hear Leonard give a speech in Brighton. "Like a foreign town: the first spring day. Women sitting on seats. A pretty hat in a teashop—how fashion revives the eye!" She recommits to Henry James's command to "observe perpetually." Like Sontag she imagines a future, a prescription for old Virginia: "Suppose I bought a ticket at the Museum; biked in daily and read history . . . Occupation is essential." "And now," she concludes, "with some pleasure I find that it's seven; and must cook dinner. Haddock and sausage meat. I think it is true that one gains a certain hold on sausage and haddock by writing them down."

III.

A friend of mine told me her journals are not retrospective, a record of time past—instead, they look forward, a record of plans and ideas and projections, sources of excitement and hope. I once wrote in a notebook, "I hate hope, and yet . . ." (And yet what—I need it? I don't believe in free will, but I can't help behaving as though I have it. In that sense, free will is automatic. It springs eternal.) I once wrote in a notebook, "Underlining books makes me want to return to them and reminds me of hiding 'treasure' (coins or candy) in my room as a kid, to forget and find later." I think I use notebooks for the same reason, as a way of hiding "treasure" for myself, for old E. I record events sometimes, date the entries sometimes—on September 25, 2021, I wrote: "I remember, the night before John's father died, they said, *He's doing a little better. He ate all his peaches.*" On September 15, 2021, I wrote: "I'm starting to remember the bleakness of 2020 fondly—well, not the bleakness exactly, but the moments of non-bleakness—making a lot of banana bread. Huddling around a kerosene camp heater on Mike's balcony. Xmas." To be more exact, I recorded the memories, not the events. (Woolf, in 1933: "It's a queer thing that I write a date. Perhaps in this disoriented life one thinks, if I can say what day it is, then . . . Three dots to signify I don't know what I mean.") But mostly they're undated, mostly they are thoughts out of nowhere. In 2021, according to my notebooks, I thought a lot about Sartre's bad faith, or mauvaise foi—the moments when we recognize the anguish of our freedom, which he called "negative ecstasy." Kierkegaard called it "the dizziness of freedom," those glimpses of the way out of the trap. Why do we always look away and never take that path out? I wrote "INERTIA & UNCERTAINTY" in all caps at the top of a page. I wrote "THIS CONNECTION BETWEEN JOURNALS & MEMORY." I put asterisks next to the interesting thoughts, the thoughts that wanted more thinking, a map to the treasure. Proof that thoughts were had. The disconnected thoughts are always me, are they not? Proof of continuity? "In the diary you find proof," Kafka writes, "that this right hand moved then as it does today." We need proof of our lives, and we need it while we live.

I wrote in August, as shorthand, "Memory—New Orleans." I know what I meant by this. When I was nineteen years old, I went to Mardi Gras with my brother, my roommate, and several other college friends and got as drunk as I've ever been, so insensibly drunk that I famously spiked a frozen hurricane, which according to most recipes already has four ounces of rum, with more rum from a flask, and blacked out standing up, such that I recall coming to in the arms of a stranger wearing skull beads. The beads were little skulls, memento mori. Later I looked so green in the very long line for the bathroom at Café du Monde that they let me skip to the front. I don't remember getting back to the hotel that night. The next day, my roommate, who was sharing a bed with me, told me that I'd puked on the sheets, so she'd yanked them off the bed and thrown them into the bathtub, and when she'd tried to pull the little decorative coverlet over us for warmth, I had told her, "They don't wash those." I swear this was the first time I ever heard that hotels don't wash the coverlets—when my friend told me *I* had told *her* so. My drunken mind had knowledge I didn't. When I told John this story, he didn't seem surprised. I guess when you're so drunk you aren't even there, you really are someone different. (Dot dot dot.)

A Complicating Energy

There's a particular stranger from deep in my past I remember. I was six years old, in a playroom at some kind of day camp. I saw a pretty brunette girl, who struck me as older and more sophisticated than I was, though she couldn't have been more than seven or eight. She was standing with friends, and I wasn't. "Do you have a staring problem?" she said, meeting my gaze. I was shocked, ashamed—and understood I should not look at people for long. But I still stare at strangers; I still have a staring problem.

I used to see strangers every day, when I commuted to an office on a train. Often, I couldn't get a seat, and though I always carried a book, I rarely opened it. The trips were short, the trains were full, and I was never bored. I spent the time looking at the other passengers—their outfits, what they were reading; the interesting neutrality of their train expressions, unrevealing of their interiors. I can't recall any one person I saw on these train rides, but I do remember patterns. Women with still-wet hair, even in winter. Men with T-shirts visible under their dress shirts. Children hovering near their parents' knees, unable to get their attention.

When I started working from home, I didn't miss seeing my coworkers, exactly, at least not as specific people. But I found I missed seeing people in general. I missed the strangers on the train. So I'd wander around a mall after work, or go to concerts or museums. (Friday night openings are barely about the art; they're about looking good in public.) In his 1712 essay "Twenty-Four Hours in London," the Irish playwright and politician Richard Steele writes, "I could not believe any Place more entertaining than Covent-Garden; where I strolled from one Fruit-Shop to another, with Crowds of agreeable young Women around me, who were purchasing Fruit for their respective Families." The eighteenth-century convention of capitalizing nouns transforms these "Women" with their "Fruit" into platonic ideals, or perhaps generic objects; it's as if he were delighted by their sameness, their interchangeability.

To people-watch, says Baudelaire, is "to see the world, to be at the centre of the world, and yet to remain hidden from the world"—to become interchangeable, one of the strangers. For Virginia Woolf, a wander through the city at dusk was an escape from the trap of being "tethered to a single mind," from the oppression of self: "The evening hour, too, gives us the irresponsibility which darkness and lamplight bestow. We are no longer quite ourselves." "Let us dally a little longer," she writes, "be content still with surfaces only"—strangers are all surface, and if we accessed their depths, they'd cease to be strangers. We're all surface to them too—all face. Strangers allow us, in a way we can't at home, or when alone, to be mysterious, unknown.

During the early pandemic, I didn't see enough faces. My dreams became crowded, creating company for me.

I'd go to dream parties and talk to old friends—sometimes very old friends, people I haven't been in touch with for decades—and make out with dream strangers. (I heard once that the strangers you see in your dreams are all real people from your past, people you have passed on the street or in other fleeting encounters, but how could you ever prove this?) A writer I know told me she had been searching for faces online so she could work on her novel: "I've never had to do this before! But it's like I can't see my characters anymore. I can't remember the tiny details people have on their faces."

I used to read a blog by the psychologist Seth Roberts, where he documented the results of elaborate self-experiments in optimizing his life and daily habits: to maintain a lower weight, to achieve better sleep and better moods. One of the odder things he discovered was what he called "morning faces therapy": "If I see faces in the morning, I feel better the next day." It's as though people have a basic need to see other people, a bodily requirement, like a recommended daily allowance of humanity. Roberts believed he could satisfy this need by watching talking heads on TV or YouTube, but I'm not so sure. I think we need faces that can see us too.

One day I saw a letter from a reader in *The Baltimore Sun*. "My 8-year-old was sobbing last night because she misses playing with her friends at recess, she misses her teacher, and she is worried that everyone has forgotten her," this mother wrote. The next part made me gasp: "*At one point she asked me if she was even real anymore.*" I felt profound recognition with this child's crisis. The self cannot be too much with itself, it seems. Trapped alone all the time, it escapes by dissolving. We *need* to be seen or we feel transparent, even nonexistent.

For much of the summer of 2020, I had a near-constant headache, and some other sensation I couldn't describe, not even to myself. I tried to tell people what it felt like, but it was as if I had a tumor in the exact part of my brain that would have given me the language to define it. The sensation was in my head, mostly, but it was separate from the pain. It felt related to lightheadedness, but it wasn't lightheadedness; it might have been the opposite. Sometimes I felt like my brain was a little too big for my skull, or that it was ringing, the way ears can ring—or reverberating, like when you accidentally bite down hard on the tines of a metal fork.

I'd been having insomnia on and off, as I always have, but one week, my sleep was disrupted in disturbing new ways. I would start to drift off, then be jolted awake as if someone had stabbed an adrenaline syringe into my heart. I had the terrifying thought that if I did fall asleep I would die, and that my body somehow knew this and was trying to keep me alive. The next day, exhausted, I described this in very vague terms to a woman I work with. She asked me if it felt like I was being electrocuted from the inside. I was stunned. It *had* felt like that. After our phone call I googled something like "electric shock feeling while falling asleep." I found an article about "brain zaps," which are typically a symptom of withdrawal from antidepressants. But I have never taken antidepressants. Could I be in withdrawal from my own normal brain chemistry, I wondered, my prepandemic levels of serotonin and endorphins? My intrinsic antidepressants? I googled the symptoms of morphine with-drawal. Anxiety, rapid heart rate, troubled sleeping—they sounded like the symptoms of anything.

Finally, after weeks of idle worrying, I made a telehealth appointment with my doctor. She thought it sounded like anxiety, but she had me come into the office for blood work and ordered a series of tests, just in case. I was sure there was something else wrong with me, something much worse—cancer, cirrhosis. In bed at night, I sobbed into my husband's shirt in fear. But everything came back normal. My doctor prescribed a beta-blocker to take before sleep, and the panicky feeling in my chest went away, for the most part. The weird sensation in my skull began to recede.

At the time, I was immersed in what I thought of as the "literature of despair." (I'd started talking to myself, not out loud but in my head; I could not stop attempting to convert my life into language.) I read William Styron's *Darkness Visible*, the novelist's memoir of his suicidal depression. "Depression is a disorder of mood," Styron writes, "so mysteriously painful and elusive in the way it becomes known to the self—to the mediating intellect—as to verge close to being beyond description." While Styron is in France to receive a major prize, he experiences "a sensation close to, but indescribably different from, actual pain." *Oh*, I thought. *I see. This pain that can't be named is well established.* But Styron, while he was afflicted, didn't understand it either. He felt a vague "internal doom" that drove him to the doctor for weeks of "high-tech and extremely expensive" tests, which deemed him "totally fit."

Charlotte Brontë suffered much from loneliness and the frustration of "unfulfilled literary ambitions," the critic

Brian Dillon notes in *Suppose a Sentence*, but she described her own malady as "hypochondria." This, he writes, "did not mean, or did not mean only, what it does today," but rather referred to a melancholic condition that we now call depression or anxiety. "Hypochondria," etymologically, means "under the sternal cartilage"—Victorian physicians believed there was some digestive component of this condition that gave the sufferer "a visionary or exaggerated sense of pain," in the words of Thomas John Graham's *Modern Domestic Medicine* manual of 1826. The contemporary sense of hypochondria, "unfounded belief that one is sick," is a linguistic narrowing, and clearly pejorative: you think you are sick, but it's all in your head, and not in your sternum.

In 2019, a woman in Cardiff, Wales, noticed an elderly man sitting alone in a busy city park for forty minutes and wondered if he wanted to talk to someone. Everyone else was walking right past him. She came up with an idea to tie signs reading HAPPY TO CHAT to certain benches. If you sat on a HAPPY TO CHAT bench, strangers could approach and sit down without worrying they might be bothering you. "All of a sudden, you're not invisible anymore," the woman said. The benches became popular in parks all over the world. They solved a problem of fear, the fear of scaring other people if you just want some contact or conversation—a fear that seems to increase when we're older, when people seem more afraid of us. (In her essay "Pause," the poet Mary Ruefle laments the loss of the human gaze after menopause: "They have looked you over to assess how attractive or unattractive you are, so no matter what the case, you were

looked at. Those days are over; now others look straight
through you, you are completely invisible to them, you have
become a ghost.")

For decades, the size of the average household in the
United States has been going down, and more and more
people are living alone. Not everyone who's alone feels
lonely, but subjective, self-reported feelings of loneliness
have increased as well. In 1985, the General Social Survey,
which measures trends in American behavior and attitudes,
began asking participants how many people they discussed
"important matters" with. That year, the most common
response to the question "How many confidants do you
have?" was three. In 2004, the most common response was
none. According to the neuroscientist John T. Cacioppo
and the editor William Patrick, the authors of *Loneliness:
Human Nature and the Need for Social Connection*, roughly
one in five people "feel sufficiently isolated for it to be a
major source of unhappiness in their lives."

This much unhappiness seems bad enough in itself,
but loneliness also has startling effects on physical health.
Your body interprets long periods of solitude—unwanted
solitude in particular; your body knows the difference—as
acutely dangerous. It activates the body's generic stress
response, causing widespread inflammation, along with
cardiovascular and immune system damage. You go into a
state of heightened awareness called "hypervigilance." Your
sympathetic nervous system switches on, causing surges
in catecholamines, like epinephrine, and cortisol, a stress
hormone that raises your blood sugar and blood pressure,
in case you need to fight or flee. It makes you feel afraid.
This response is adaptive in an actual emergency, but not

sustainable over time. Social isolation increases your risk of premature death from any cause by roughly 25 percent, a level comparable to hypertension or smoking. (Some of these loneliness-associated deaths are simply the result of no one being around to help you.) It accelerates aging. And it hurts, in the most basic sense—even over-the-counter painkillers can be moderately effective in treating symptoms of depression and loneliness, since they're anti-inflammatory. My brain may indeed have gotten slightly too big for my skull.

Of course, most lonely people aren't aware all this is happening in their bodies, in the dark. They just feel *bad*. In a 2013 poll, three-fourths of general practitioners in the UK claimed they saw at least one patient per day whose visit was driven primarily by loneliness. I suspect this goes both ways—my father is an internist, and at seventy-four he was reluctant to stop working, since his practice was his main source of social life, his office the main place he saw anyone he knew apart from my mother. A number of his patients had been seeing him for thirty or forty years, and some had begged him not to retire until they died. One had been his first-grade teacher—up until her death, he still called her "Mrs. Baird." My father finally shut down his practice in 2020; given his age, and my mother's delicate health, it wasn't practical, or safe, to keep it open.

All animals have an innate "sociality" level, and humans are considered "obligatorily gregarious," like the apes we evolved from. According to Cacioppo, apes spend a good 10 percent of their time engaged in grooming one another, and "cleaning fur is the least of it"—"the more important objective is to promote troop harmony and cohesion." (I remember, when I was in fourth and fifth grade, it was common for girls to play with one another's hair, a kind of group bonding activity. It was a feeling I loved; I miss it.) Biologists believe that loneliness may have evolved as a signal analogous to hunger or thirst, the body's way of increasing conscious urgency: You *must* eat, you *must* drink. We also *must* be around people some of the time—to feel good, yes, but also just to feel normal, like we can get through the day.

Pets go some way toward easing loneliness—elderly people with pets go to the doctor less often. I read an article in NPR about people whose hair was falling out in clumps from all the stress, or whose teeth were cracking from grinding their jaws at night. It suggested "staring into a pet's eyes" could help release a hormone to counteract inflammation. The companionship must help too, having a warm, soft body to touch. I'm allergic to cats and dogs— all the warm, soft mammals—and I have no children, but during the early pandemic, I sometimes dreamed I had a kitten or a baby. A pet has a face that sees you.

In a graphic essay called "What Do We Lose When We Stop Touching Each Other?" the writer and illustrator Kristen Radtke describes moving to a "driving city" at age twenty-five, a city "strung with interstates and very few sidewalks." In this environment, "there was no accidental touching"—"no stumbling into another body when the bus jerked to a stop, no brushing a shoulder as I passed someone on the sidewalk." She was living alone—without touching strangers, she touched no one at all.

In another essay, Radtke describes asking people what

they missed most about touch during the pandemic. Someone responded: "I used to wash hair at a salon. One woman would moan slightly when I touched her head. She found ways to extend her hair-washing time, which I was already extending because she obviously needed it. One day she told me, 'My husband is dead and I have no children or grandchildren; you're the only one who touches me.'" Another missed the moment of prayer in AA meetings: "At the end of a 12-step meeting, we stand and grab the hands of strangers or friends on either side of us." Alcoholics Anonymous is heavily influenced by Christian traditions, and I remember doing something similar in high school, when I went to church sometimes with my Catholic best friend. My Protestant family rarely went to church, and I always felt shy during this moment, an impostor. (Religious people live longer lives, but only if they attend religious services, suggesting it's the gatherings that matter and not the spirituality. Similarly, AA is much less effective if you don't attend the meetings.) In a third piece, Radtke notes that receiving regular hugs has been shown to ease symptoms of the flu. Isolation reduces your chances of contracting a virus, but it may make your illness feel worse, and last longer, if you do get sick. "Part of the unfairness of loneliness," Cacioppo writes, "is that it often deprives us of touch." Psychologists call this need for touch "skin hunger."

Before 2020, if your skin hunger got intense, you could hire a professional cuddler. I watched a video profile of one professional cuddler who noted that talk therapy is helpful for loneliness—which is similar in some ways to depression but not identical—but "conventional therapists are not allowed to touch their clients," so "touch-deprived people" may need a different service. The next video served up by the YouTube algorithm was a BuzzFeed video called "People Spoon with Professional Cuddlers for the First Time." I watched that too. In these videos, the professionals, many of them employed by a company called Cuddlist, talk through the process. First, you have to sign an agreement that the encounter will remain nonsexual. Then, you do an activity called "companioning"—just sitting side by side for a bit, not touching. Dramatic music plays over the cuddling footage. A woman in a blue shirt tells her cuddler, or "cuddlist," "I always wanted a sister growing up, and so, like, I love it when people play with my hair, because it feels like having a sister."

In another video, titled "I Am a Professional Cuddler for a Living," Christina Hepburn says, "America is kind of starved for touch, especially in big cities . . . You see it a lot where people are living by themselves now, often without family." Hence "your touch needs aren't being met." Hepburn's sessions are very consent based, with lots of questions: Can I put my head on your shoulder? Can I touch your feet? She talks about her favorite poses, some almost contortions—such as lying back to back—and places to touch people, nonobvious places like earlobes and inside the ears. (John is much taller than me, and I like, when I hug him, to fit his Adam's apple into the hollow between my nose and eye, a nook that seems made for it.) Hepburn says "cuddling is life-affirming." Watching these videos, I kept recalling specific times I'd been touched in the past. I remembered a school assembly, in second or third grade, when a boy's shirt brushed against my arm, giving me chills. I remembered sitting on the balcony at a party, in my twenties, when the man I had a crush on came outside and rested his palm on the top of my head. Aimee Bender once described that, a palm on the head, as "the heaviest, best hat." I sometimes think touch on the face or the head is the most memorable kind of touch—perhaps because our selfhood is located there. It seems to emanate from there, behind my eyes.

What has happened to the professional cuddling industry, I wondered? What about massage parlors—an incredibly common and socially acceptable way to exchange money for touch from a stranger? From time to time that year I wondered this, about some industry or other—life changed in many ways I didn't keep up with. I checked the Cuddlist website and it said they were offering virtual sessions, which sort of made me want to cry, even though I had someone to touch me in person for free.

For writers, isolation can represent a kind of glamour. We need time and space to write, of course, but not total, extended isolation. If Woolf wanted a room of her own, she also wanted to "step out of the house on a fine evening between four and six," to join the "army of anonymous trampers, whose society is so agreeable after the solitude." This is how most writing residencies work: a communal meal after your day of writing. A communal reward. According to Cacioppo, "the lining of the digestive system" is similar to the skin, and "eating serves as a kind of internal massage" that releases oxytocin. Plus, "moderate amounts of alcohol increase the concentration of oxytocin in the blood," which

explains why eating and drinking with people is so enjoy-
able. I almost think of it as a hobby—more of a hobby than
writing, which is more like a second job.

For most people, social activity isn't just nice to have.
Isolation disrupts our cognitive functioning and inhibits
concentration—lonely people have an attentional deficit—
and while the state of hypervigilance makes us more at-
tuned to social cues, it also makes us more inclined to
misinterpret them. It reduces our empathy, or, you might
say, it weakens our theory of mind. We get worse at imagining other people's emotions and motivations. These effects make it difficult to focus, difficult to make good use
of our alone time. Tragically, they also make it harder to
make friends.

Reading a volume of *Paris Review* interviews, I noticed
every time that a writer mentioned strangers. Here's Joyce
Carol Oates, in 1987: "I like to . . . stroll around shopping
malls and observe the qualities of people, overhearing
snatches of conversations, noting people's appearance, their
clothes, and so forth. Walking and driving a car are part
of my life as a writer, really." Jean Rhys in 1979: "Week
after week, if you never see anyone, it can become trying.
If there's a knock at the door, I expect some wonderful
stranger. I fly to the door. But it's only the postman." (I
feel the same every time I hear my email ding. Is it a major
award? No, it's a LinkedIn notification.) And Ted Hughes,
who was interested in tarot, Ouija, the occult, in 1995:

> Goethe couldn't write a line if there was another per-
> son anywhere in the same house, or so he said . . . My

feeling is that your sense of being concentrated can deceive you . . . Fast asleep, we keep track of the time to the second. The person conversing at one end of a long table quite unconsciously uses the same unusual words, within a second or two, as the person conversing with someone else at the other end—though they're amazed to learn they've done it.

I think Hughes is right. We may think we need to be alone, but we get some kind of subconscious energy from strangers and from crowds, a complicating energy that produces ideas. They may not be our own ideas exactly, but they feel unfamiliar and therefore more original, at least to ourselves.

In one of the multiple group chats I've become part of since the pandemic started (which some days accounted for my only social interaction outside of conversations with John), a writer asked, "When do you feel most free?" One of us answered, "When I'm traveling all day—like in the beforetimes, you know? Twelve straight hours of airplanes and airports . . . obviously you lose a lot of freedom that way (where to sit, what to eat) but you also get to just sort of be a brain in a jar and read/listen to music for a million hours straight cuz there's nothing else to do." Another replied, "I was going to say: a delayed flight and Bloody Mary at an airport bar, half reading and half watching other passengers."

I didn't miss flying exactly, but at one point I read a book with a scene in a train station and felt a desperate longing to be in that scene—to have some time to kill, to drink a glass of champagne in a transit bar, alone but not alone. Why is that setting so conducive to thinking? Those are the interludes when I write in my notebook, when my mind is most alive.

The year dragged on. In the summer, when it wasn't too hot, and when the air quality wasn't too dangerous—drought, wildfires, and industrial air pollution now make Denver one of the ten worst US cities to breathe in—I'd go for long walks through nearby neighborhoods. I thought of these as "my constitutionals," my old-timey self-care. Denverites are always extravagant with outdoor seasonal decor, but they were even more so in 2020, and I watched the yard decorations change from lingering Christmas lights, to Black Lives Matter signs, to Halloween fantasias (giant animatronic spiders, lots of fake graveyards), to Christmas again, starting earlier this time.

Often, on these walks, I passed a mixed-use complex, still under construction, with apartments or condos on the upper floors and retail space below. It sat half completed all year; a CVS and a coffee shop were open, but a movie theater and most of the other storefronts were empty, and some didn't have flooring yet. (I called all of these "the dirt store" in my head.) They looked like ruins from another era, as if I were a tourist in an ancient city. But when I saw people in the café, eating and chatting normally, it felt more like they were alive and I was dead, like Emily from *Our Town*. They felt far away.

This isn't life, I heard someone say, in early lockdown—a maddening remark, since dying on a ventilator isn't life either. But I think I know what they meant—that the sameness every day, the lack of new faces, was like dreamless sleep, like lost time, not experienced life. Commuting is life, with the strangers on the train. Covent Garden is life.

It was early winter when people started getting vaccines. There were signs of spring when my parents got theirs—crocus buds in melting snow. During that period of waiting, I missed everyone, everyone I knew and didn't know. Yet, and this is something that I can't explain, I sometimes caught myself fearing that things would all go back to normal too soon, and I wouldn't be ready. Why would I fear that, when I hated that way of living? My soul was glitching.

Infinite Abundance on a Narrow Ledge

Notes on Rilke, Architecture, and Mental Space

If I remember anything about a book, I also remember where I read it—what room, what chair. I read most of Rilke's poetry while sitting by a north-facing window in our apartment in Denver, early mornings in 2020 when I woke before dawn and couldn't get back to sleep. I couldn't see the sun rise from there, but I could see the sky turn from black to dusky blue—the dusk of morning—and then pink. The sort of corridor between our building and the brick house next door would seem to fill with warm pink light, a glorious light with unnatural substance. I wanted to touch it. The effect lasted fifteen minutes or so, a brief interval of glow in the day that I passed through alone.

A few poems I read in the sun, on our friend's back porch. She and her husband and kids had fled north to be with family who could help out with childcare while they worked. Every few days, John and I would drive to their house and sit on the porch, late summer afternoons and evenings, and share a bottle of white wine while reading, a pencil on the table between us so we could underline and asterisk our books. I didn't use to like pencils, or writing in books, but John does, and now I do too. I like to dog-ear favorite poems in a book of poetry, a cheat code for the future, so when I pull out a book that I haven't touched in years, it tells me where to go. My whole experience of a book, any book, is spatial. For years sometimes, I remember which side, verso or recto, my favorite parts appeared on, how deep in the book, how far down the page. A book always feels like a place I've been to.

Rilke conceived of the world in terms of shapes and expanses, interiors and exteriors. Existence and nonexistence were spatial—places you could be. In his only novel, *The Notebooks of Malte Laurids Brigge*, a novel that draws from his real correspondence, and which he almost called *The Journal of My Other Self*, he writes of a young man learning to live, to be and to see. "The main thing was, being alive. That was the main thing." Selfhood is constructed here, a place to see from: "I have an interior now that I never knew of," Malte writes in his notebook. A vestibule, a corridor, a lookout. "Everything passes into it now."

In this Proustian novel (it's like Proust, but short) Malte, who is certainly a stand-in for Rainer, is driven by the horrors he sees on Paris streets deep into his own mind, his past. He is haunted by memories of strange encounters with the uncanny, with deaths (his father, a dog) and refusals to die. On these occasions, there's an apprehension of the flimsy partition between our world and the other, the finite and the infinite. The dead don't not exist, for Rilke; nonexistence is existence elsewhere. In one remarkable passage, Malte recounts "the story of 'the hand,'" a story the character once almost told to his mother, but he hesitated, then the moment passed. "So, strangely enough, this is the first time I am telling (and after all only for myself) about

an event that now lies far back in my childhood." ("Only
for myself," the notebook reads, yet it often feels that Rilke,
through Malte, is speaking directly to you, to me, through
time. It is that conversational: "Have I already said that he
was blind? No? Well, he was blind.")

In this memory of "the hand," young Malte is drawing
in a dark room; his red crayon rolls off the table. "I can see
it now," Rilke writes—Malte is watching his memory like a
film, projected in 3D. In the void beneath the table: "I didn't
know what belonged to me and what was the chair's . . . The
darkness seemed so dense that I was afraid I would knock
against it." When his eyes begin to adjust, his own hand
appears alien, crab-like, to him: "It seemed to know things
I had never taught it." Then, most terribly, he sees another
hand, "groping in a similar fashion from the other side . . .
I felt that one of the hands belonged to me and that it was
about to enter into something it could never return from."
The child has no words for this experience, but he has a
premonition of a later understanding: "The fear seized me
that nevertheless, beyond my years, these words would all
at once be there, and what seemed to me the most horrible thing of all was that I would then have to say them."
This brush with the void is too much for young Malte, who
is fearful and delicate like the child in Proust: "I see myself lying in my little bed, unable to sleep, and somehow
vaguely foreseeing that life would be like that: full of truly
strange experiences that are meant for one person alone and
can never be spoken." They must stay *inside*. And much,
much later, these unsayable memories still evoke real fright.
When we "wake up gasping" from a nightmare, a candle
with its "half-bright solace" offers comfort, but "what a

narrow ledge" it stands on. "Beware of the light that makes space more hollow," he writes. "You are already almost outside yourself and can't get back in."

The first page of the novel, this fictional notebook, has a date and location: "*September 11th, rue Toullier.*" This is the street Rilke actually lived on when he was in Paris on commission for a work about Rodin. There are no other dates in the book. Are we to believe all these thoughts spilled out in one day, that the words did come "all at once"? I don't read it that way—it seems to me more of a path into the structure that the novel then abandons, a mimed door we never see again. But it would make a kind of sense, since Rilke viewed time as illusion, as paradox. In memory, in writing, "Everything is here. Everything forever." Moments are eternal. How, Malte wonders, when we think of our childhood, do we "reconcile the length of those days with the brevity of life"? And memories remembered unattach themselves from time: "The fact that they were past made them almost arise as future." Of his grandfather Count Brahe, Malte writes in his notebook: "The passing of time had absolutely no meaning for him; death was a minor incident which he completely ignored; people whom he had once installed in his memory continued to exist, and the fact that they had died did not alter that in the least."

Rilke, in his lifetime, wrote many condolence letters, and all espouse a view of death as transformation rather than loss. They are, I find, persuasively consoling. He believed the dead live on in us. In one letter he wrote: "There is death in life, and it astonishes me that we pretend to ignore this: death, whose unforgiving presence we experience with each change we survive because we must learn to die slowly. We must learn to die: That is all of life." Death, you might say, is the point of life—or life is the point of death. In another, he wrote: "Does the person who passes away not leave all the things he had begun in hundreds of ways to be continued by those who outlive him?" For Rilke, the death of a loved one creates obligation—or more so, opportunity. When our parents die we lose that sense of sacred protection, but we become protectors, like angels, ourselves. That is our sacred inheritance—death bestows honor on those who still live. (I've just noticed, reading Rilke, that "still" can refer to duration in time—still alive—and duration, as an object, in space. To be still.) In another: "You *must* continue his life *inside* of yours . . . All of our true relationships, all of our enduring experiences touch upon and pass through *everything*, Sidie, through life and death. *We must live in both*." Another: "Transience is not separation." Another:

> The distance between birth and death above which we write "I" is not a measure for God; life & death constitute for him probably only a small degree of separation, and perhaps a continual series of lives and deaths is needed for God to have the impression: one. Perhaps only all of creation in its totality is permitted to call itself "I" before him.

The distance between, that small degree—we live on a narrow ledge. There's an essay by Freud called "On Transience," in which he takes a walk through the meadows with an unnamed poet, who is often presumed to be Rilke. This "pessimistic poet," Freud writes, "admired the beauty of nature around us, but without enjoying it . . . Everything he would otherwise have loved and admired seemed to him devalued by the transience for which it was fated." Surely this poet could not have been Rilke, unless Freud had strongly misread him.

In *The Poetics of Space*, Gaston Bachelard thinks a lot about Rilke, quoting from his poetry and prose. He notes Rilke's obsession with furniture and things—so often, but not always, *Things*—the significance of insignificant objects. "For the sake of a single poem," Malte writes, "you must see many cities, many people and Things." "Familiar, intimate Things." "Things vibrate into one another . . . Every flower is everywhere." These life objects, the objects of our lives, have mythical, mystical significance. They contain life. They are "filled with significance, through and through." In another condolence letter, Rilke wondered if his was the last generation to truly appreciate things, things which were once more transient, more irreplaceable, and therefore more precious than we can grasp. (The older I get, the more interest I have in old knickknacks, no matter how randomly acquired, the bric-a-brac from dead people's shelves. These *Things* are technically worthless, but they do have history, a glow of life—a precarious worthlessness that gives them value.)

Bachelard notes Rilke's interest in boxes, in corners, in wardrobes, in locks and keys, in doors as magical portals. In one passage from the novel—it's a dreamy, passage-driven novel—Malte describes a room from his childhood whose walls were paneled with "deep, gray wardrobes," one of which contained a key that opened all the others. In the wardrobes he finds wondrous costumes, or regular clothes that are costumes to him: "What transported me into a kind of intoxication were the spacious cloaks, the scarves, the shawls, the veils," lace and silk and ribbons, and masks—"I had never seen any masks before," he confesses, "but I immediately understood that masks ought to exist."

These wardrobe doors are portals to the other self, the mask or the costume that permits transformation. In Bachelard's terms, a door is a "cosmos of the half-open." *Half* because it isn't so easy to slip through these portals, between dreams and life, between space and time. "Memory—what a strange thing it is!—does not record concrete duration, in the Bergsonian sense of the word," Bachelard writes. "We are unable to relive duration that has been destroyed." Why is this, I wonder? Because reliving it during our present would lead to a double duration— too much time to fit? "We can only think of it," Bachelard writes, that already lived time, "in the line of an abstract time that is deprived of all thickness." The narrowest ledge. He quotes from Rilke's *Cahiers*, a sentence that also appears in *The Notebooks of Malte Laurids Brigge*: "And there is almost no space here; and you feel almost calm at the thought that it is impossible for anything very large to hold in this narrowness."

I have a memory of a house that I fantasized about as a child, a tiny child-size house. "An oneiric house, a house of dream-memory," Bachelard would say. In my fantasy it had the same fireplace as the real house I lived in, the fireplace around which sparkling gifts appeared—they seemed that way to me, to sparkle with impossibility—on Christmas mornings, but in my house, my version of the house, the one room was cylindrical, so I could sit in the middle, with everything in reach. During those years I had an armchair in my bedroom, a recliner with soft blue upholstery, that sat in the corner, and my habit was to sit behind the armchair on the floor, in the tentlike space that was formed by the tilted back of the chair and the walls. I am not sure how I had enough light to read in this makeshift room, with the chair looming overhead and blocking any light from the window, but I know that I did this. I prefer to read in winter, because reading is improved by cozy conditions—under blankets with a fire is best, a candle if no fireplace is present. As Bachelard notes, snow makes houses cozier. The blanket of white makes the outside world, the "non-house," into a "simplified cosmos."

I remembered that nook that I'd made of the chair, that nook for my self, one weekend in my midtwenties, when I stayed at a house in Vermont that belonged to the aunt of a friend in my cohort at grad school. The aunt had invited a few of us up for a writing retreat, of a kind; we were preparing our graduate theses. I think I believed that my thesis, a collection of poems, was already done, but I wanted to go to Vermont. (I recently reread that thesis, in the course of cleaning files off a laptop I needed to get rid of; it was dreadful.) I had some time to kill in the afternoons, while the other poets were dutifully working. It was snowy outside and warm inside. The house had a beautiful library, and I pulled a thick hardcover book off the built-in shelves, curled up in a chair, and skim-read as much as I could in a couple of hours. The book was *A Pattern Language*, published in 1977, by the architect Christopher Alexander and a group of his colleagues at Berkeley.

For a long time I wanted to be an architect—it couldn't have been very long, but childhood years feel longer—which must have been what attracted me to the book, which I later bought for myself. (Technically I bought it for John as a gift, which justified the high price, but I bought it for myself.) The book is a set of 253 "patterns." Some are about city planning, the uses of public space, the patterns of towns and communities ("ARCADES"—"PROMENADE"—"BUS STOP"—"BEER HALL"), and others are about the home, the uses of private space ("THE FLOW THROUGH ROOMS"—"SHORT PASSAGES"—"CHILDREN'S REALM"). There are patterns of towns ("LACE OF COUNTRY STREETS"—"NETWORK OF LEARNING") and patterns of buildings ("ROOF VAULTS"—"ALCOVES"—"MARRIAGE BED"—"WINDOW PLACE"). As Alexander writes in the introduction, "Each pattern describes a problem which occurs over and over again in our environment, and then describes the core of the solution to that problem, in such a way that you can use this solution a million times over, without ever doing it the same way twice." The book is meant to empower regular people, not just architects, to manipulate and influence the spaces they live and work in, to design their own houses. (Of course, before there were professional architects, people did this all the time.) It is meant to be adapted, like open-source code. The patterns are "archetypal"—they address basic human desires: "SMALL PUBLIC SQUARES." "DANCING IN THE STREET." "OLD PEOPLE EVERYWHERE." "CHILDREN IN THE CITY." And they are meant to be used together: "The building is very dense; it has many meanings captured in a small space; and through this density, it becomes profound."

In Alexander's view, the aesthetics of cities and buildings go far beyond aesthetics. Certain features of buildings— "ceiling height variety," "windows overlooking life"—and towns—unplanned encounters with strangers—are vitally necessary to happiness, or not even happiness. They are part of humanity, of being okay. We need them, and buildings that deprive us of these elements are prisons, they are cursed. If we ignore these patterns, or solve the problems incorrectly, we risk suffering, illness, death. "There is abundant evidence to show that high buildings make people crazy," he writes, arguing for a four-story limit in cities, citing studies that show adolescents who live in a high-rise are "socially deprived" and more prone to ennui. (It is true that people on the upper floors of buildings are more likely to die of a heart attack, because, quite simply, they can't receive medical help as quickly.)

The evidence is useful, if sometimes dubious, but as in philosophy, it's the force of sensibility that convinces you he's right or he isn't. I've been convinced for twenty years that much of what he argues is right. He argues that grave sites should be closer to the living: "No people who turn their backs on death can be alive. The presence of the dead among the living will be a daily fact in any society which encourages its people to live." This is so Rilkean, so true. "The small graveyards which once put people into daily contact with the fact of death, have vanished—replaced by massive cemeteries, far away from people's daily business." In downtown Boston there are tiny ancient graveyards stuck between the newer buildings, headstones right next to the coffee shops. You can't walk from work to the train down there without passing a grave. In El Paso, where I grew up, I never passed a cemetery walking, only in a car, on the way out of town. (You were supposed to hold your breath, but the graveyards were too vast to do that.)

Alexander writes that the "realms" in a building complex "must have *names*"—"this requires, in turn that they be well enough defined physically, so that they can in fact be named." Without named realms for the maps in our minds we get lost and disoriented—we must treat any space like a kingdom. Building-building is world-building. He writes that towns need animals, such as chickens and goats and bees—they are "as important a part of nature as the trees and grass and flowers." This is so true. I feel so much better when I go on a hike and see a moose or an owl, when I go on a walk and see anything that feels like a wild animal—a hawk or a bat, a raccoon, a deer. Even a magpie or rabbit will do, even a very large dog, as long as it's rarer and larger than a squirrel. Once while driving through the mountains, John and I were having an argument, when he braked to let a fox cross the road. We stopped arguing. Seeing a fox is a very good way to end an argument.

In one pattern, Alexander writes about positive and negative outdoor spaces: "Outdoor space is negative when it is shapeless, the residue left behind," and positive "when it has a distinct and definite shape, as definite as the shape of a room." Negative space should be convex, not concave. In an environment with positive outdoor spaces, a radical reversal is possible: the buildings can become merely background to the figure of the unenclosed space. He illustrates the difference, and writes in a caption: "This space can be felt: it is distinct:—a place . . ." Of the contrasted negative space, he writes: "This space is vague, amorphous, 'nothing.'" We prefer to be enclosed on some level; it's why public squares need something "roughly in the middle," a statue or a fountain, "where people can protect their backs." In a wide-open space we are vulnerable (lightning, assassins!), naked before God and hostile alien invaders. Positive space will be used and enjoyed, but people neglect a negative space; they don't even see it as usable space.

This need for enclosure is why children love "tiny, cave-like places," and why adults too need a "secret place," a place where "the need for concealment" can be expressed, "the need for something precious to be lost, and then revealed." He quotes Bachelard on the magic of "wardrobes with their shelves, desks with their drawers, and chests with their false bottoms," places for our most precious Rilkean objects, our intimate Things. Alexander also has much to say of roofs, which must be "large and visible": "The roof plays a primal role in our lives. The most primitive buildings are nothing but a roof. If the roof is hidden, if its presence cannot be felt around the building . . . people will lack a fundamental sense of shelter." I think about this idea almost every day, almost every time I see a roof. The roof, in a way, is proof of the building. He has much to say of windows. Hallways should be short, he writes, and "as much like rooms as possible, with carpets or wood on the floor, furniture, bookshelves, beautiful windows . . . The best corridors and passages of all are those which have windows along an entire wall." Windows, like the spaces between buildings, offer chances to make places: "A 'place' is a partly enclosed, distinctly identifiable spot within a room." "Everybody loves window seats, bay windows, and big windows with low sills and comfortable chairs drawn up to them," he writes, and "windows which create 'places' next to them are not simply luxuries; they are *necessary*." We are drawn toward windows as sources of light, light that transforms hollow space to a place we can be in, a narrowness. A nook to enclose our Dasein.

In his essay "In Praise of Shadows," the Japanese writer Junichiro Tanizaki expounds at length on the power of darkness to help us appreciate light. He asks us to ponder the image of a "lonely" light bulb as seen through a shade, and then through a shoji, and then through a window, except in the opposite order, from your train seat at dusk—all those layers between you. It's an essay on the loss of true darkness to history: "The man of today, long used to electric light, has forgotten that such a darkness existed. It must have been simple for specters to appear in a 'visible darkness.'" (It was that kind of darkness—"O night without objects"—that enveloped Malte's childhood, a darkness in which phantom hands emerged from walls and houses disappeared. In *that* darkness, ghosts were utterly real.) It's an essay on the difference between Eastern and Western aesthetics—how dull the moment "when soup is served Western style, in a pale shallow bowl," compared with the serving of soup in a lacquerware bowl, by candlelight: "a moment of mystery, it might almost be called, a moment of trance." And white rice against glistening black lacquer "is a sight no Japanese can fail to be moved by." The lacquer shines best in darkness, and the darkness is improved by the lacquer:

> If the lacquer is taken away, much of the spell disappears from the dream world built by that strange light of candle and lamp, that wavering light beating the pulse of the night. Indeed the thin, impalpable, faltering light, picked up as though little rivers were running through the room, collecting little pools here and there, lacquers a pattern on the surface of the night itself.

I think Tanizaki and Christopher Alexander are saying something similar—these contrasts of inside and outside, and lightness and darkness, create little thresholds we pass through from hour to hour. These simple transitions, such as walking through a trellis, or sitting down for breakfast, can change your whole mood. A room *is* a mood, and we need different moods, small and capacious. The past is more past when it happened somewhere else, with other qualities of light. The changes are needed—they make time more felt.

Poets, like architects, love contradiction and near incoherence. "I like complexity and contradiction in architecture," the architect Robert Venturi writes in his book *Complexity and Contradiction in Architecture*. Not outright sloppiness, he's quick to note—"I do not like the incoherence or arbitrariness of incompetent architecture." (What would true incoherence look like? Maybe the Winchester Mystery House, which Sarah Winchester, heir to a firearms fortune, kept under construction until she died, an attempt to appease the ghosts of those killed by her husband's rifles. It's a nonsense house, with staircases leading up to ceilings and doors that open into thin air. I read about the house in a book as a kid, and was greatly disappointed, when we toured it on a trip to California, that the atmosphere was theme-park-like and not at all haunted.) Venturi likes a "nonstraightforward architecture" that embraces "the richness and ambiguity of modern experience." He likes Times Square and Vegas. He likes "messy vitality over obvious unity," "richness of meaning rather than clarity of meaning," things that are "boring as well as 'interesting.'" He quotes Eliot and Gödel. He likes "violent adjacencies" of scale, things that seem wildly out of proportion to their surroundings—the "colossal head of Constantine" on the side of a Roman museum, a massive mosaic of Christ on the ceiling of a Sicilian cathedral. He likes "chaotic juxtapositions" and apparent mistakes, or apparently intentional mistakes, and mistakes of history, like the "hyperproximities" of humble houses right next to grand churches in old cities. All this speaks also to poetry, to all books, I think—how much I prefer books that seem a little wrong or unfinished or somehow unprovable. Poets' novels often are messy and strange transmutations of life, chimerical objects stuck in transition between fiction and non-, one state and another. They are often disproportional, like thatched-roof houses that appear to have far too much roof for the house, like giant mushroom caps on tiny stems. I like this kind of wrongness. I think a book has to make some decisions that do feel arbitrary. "A building with no 'imperfect' part can have no perfect part," Venturi writes, "because contrast supports meaning." Ditto for books.

"Mies," he writes, of van der Rohe, "makes wonderful buildings only because he ignores many aspects of a building. If he solved more problems, his buildings would be far less potent." Le Corbusier defined the function of a house as "1. A shelter against heat, cold, rain, thieves and the inquisitive. 2. A receptacle for light and sun. 3. A certain number of cells appropriated to cooking, work, and personal life." Everything else is merely decorative, this suggests. He gave his famous Villa Savoye a flat roof that also served as a garden, a reclamation by nature of a once useless space—but was it useless, the visible roof that telegraphs roofness? He always assured his clients, according to Alain de Botton, that a flat roof is "cheaper to construct, easier to maintain and cooler in summer." But the Savoyes' roof began to leak within a week of their moving in, and their son ended up with pneumonia. In a letter to her architect, Madame Savoye wrote: "It's raining in the hall, it's raining on the ramp, and the wall of the garage is absolutely soaked." But many architects and critics loved the building, as they loved the Glass House by Philip Johnson, a transparent shoebox rejecting all typical symbols and signs of security. (Rilke, as Malte, writes, "My God, I have no roof over me, and it is raining into my eyes." I only realized late in life that *Rainer*, being German, is pronounced like Rhein-er, and not one who rains.)

When I was twenty-two and ignorant of architecture, history, and most other things, I walked into the Pantheon in Rome and was amazed to see a giant hole in the ceiling, the oculus at the top of the dome—an eye to see the sky through, or for God to look down into. Part of the shock is the contrast between the straightness of the front elevation (the architectural term for one side of a building), a big rectangular portico with a triangular pediment, and the roundness of the interior—it was constructed in such a way that if the dome could be flipped upside down, it would fit inside the building. So the space is a kind of spectral sphere, and feels larger than possible. It is still my favorite building I've ever been in. It was sunny that day, very hot, and I've always wondered what it must be like in the rain. Do they cover the hole? Or let the rain pour in? I haven't looked it up; I don't want to know if they cover it.

This is one of the contradictions Venturi speaks of—spaces that are both inside and outside—and one of Alexander's patterns—the "outdoor room." In Europe in the Middle Ages, most structures had a hole in the roof, to let out the smoke from the necessary fire. In his book *At Home*, a kind of domestic history, the author Bill Bryson marvels at "how long it took people to achieve even the most elemental levels of comfort." He notes that roof holes let out the smoke but also let in unfortunate weather. During this period houses were mostly just halls, big open spaces with fires in the middle, where people ate and slept (on beds of straw) and did anything else they did while trying to survive frequent famines and plagues. There was no word for room in English "until the time of the Tudors." And there were no second floors, because of the fires. The Normans brought fireplaces to England in the fourteenth century, but nobody liked them at first—being off to the side, they weren't nearly as warm. The fireplaces grew to be enormous, to be actual places like rooms you could be in. People even built benches inside.

Almost every book about architecture talks about fire. When I wanted to be an architect, my interest was in houses.

I collected house plans wherever I could find them—ideas of houses. Maybe what I wanted was not the career but a different house—I lived in the same house from birth until I was eighteen and moved out for college; my parents still live there—and its promise of a different life. I frequently dreamed up new houses in my sleep. I prefer to walk, if I can't be in nature, through neighborhoods with interesting houses, nicer than the ones I tend to live in. I take note of the roofs. I notice where the chimneys are and try to imagine the corresponding fireplaces. When I was twelve or so, my parents had their wood-burning fireplace converted to gas. It was the fireplace I'd put in my tiny dream house. The idea was that it would be so much easier to light and extinguish that we'd use it more often. But the fireplace lost almost all its appeal. It no longer gave off any real heat, and it didn't smell delicious—it didn't smell like anything—and worst of all, it didn't crackle. I love the sound of a wood fire, and I got through many a winter in our Denver apartment by burning a special kind of candle with a crackling wooden wick, and by playing ASMR white-noise videos on YouTube with names like "Cozy Reading Nook Ambience" and, my favorite, "Crackling Campfire on the Windy Tundra of Norway." The gas fireplace offered no drama, and after the conversion, we only used it once a year, on Christmas, and in a perfunctory fashion.

If there's a TV on in a bar, I've noticed, and there almost always is, the movement pulls your eye to it, no matter how boring what's on is. A fire is the same, but a fire is never boring. When I was shopping for a house, I ruled out all the houses with no fireplaces, though I couldn't afford any of them anyway. I wanted a fireplace with bookshelves all around it—that's what I wanted to look at. Bachelard wrote a whole book about fire, which Alexander quotes from in *A Pattern Language*: "One can hardly conceive of a philosophy of repose that would not include a reverie before a flaming log fire . . . To be deprived of a reverie before a burning fire is to lose the first use and the truly human use of fire." "There is no substitute for fire," Alexander writes. Every house needs a hearth, and a thoughtfully designed one. "The much loved and much used places in buildings, where the most things happen, are places like window seats, verandas, fireside corners, trellised arbors; all of them defined by non-uniformities in light, and all of them allowing the people who are in them to orient themselves toward the light." Or as Tanizaki writes, when considering electric heaters, "Without the red coals, the whole mood of winter is lost." We *need* fire. The interior decorator Barbara d'Arcy said, "All rooms *need* books." Fires are life objects. Books are life objects and not optional.

I obviously didn't become an architect, but I do think of writing as spatial. I think essays, like buildings, need structure and mood. The first paragraph should function as a foyer or an antechamber, bringing you into the mood. Alexander writes that a building should have a "graceful transition between the street and the inside." "If the transition is too abrupt there is no feeling of arrival." He cites a study that showed people judge houses with greater degrees of transition between inside and outside to be more "houselike," to exhibit more "houseness." The transitional space makes room for change of mood, for "ambiguous territories" and "intimacy gradients." The same could be said of essays. ("Stanza" means "room"—from Italian, for "standing place"—but paragraphs are more like rooms than stanzas are.) I like to think of a piece of writing as an environment for thinking, a semicontained space with some wandering-around room—a clearing in the woods, plus a little of the woods, or a house museum, like the Gardner in Boston, with its bright ferny courtyard in the middle, and all its smaller side rooms, baroque crowded rooms, too dark almost to see the paintings. Or Peggy Guggenheim's house in Venice, with the sculpture garden out in the back by the water. A site where interesting thoughts can happen, a site with open doors and multiple paths out. Sometimes I think of the seed of the essay, whatever idea first made me want to write it, as a tree that I'm building a house around. I knew a girl, as a child, whose father kept sex books in locked glass cabinets, and whose entrance hall was a square of wooded dirt with a skylight ceiling. Ever since I have wanted a house with a tree inside.

In the year that I read so much Rilke, I had trouble remembering books. Reading all my books in the same three rooms suspended time and erased my memories, as though there were no new hooks for them to hang on. (When I reread the Tanizaki, I barely remembered anything about it. But my pencil marks were already there, the same things I'd underline now.) I was deeply unhappy, so unhappy I believed that everyone everywhere must be unhappy. So I was surprised when a friend, a broke artist, told me that in some ways the pandemic improved his life—it suddenly seemed okay to be a broke artist, to stay home making art. A layer of shame lifted up from his life.

In another letter, Rilke writes of witnessing a suicide victim being pulled from the Seine. A passing carriage driver said to him, "So, tell me, this one, if he could still do that, he could have done something else." If he had the strength to die, that is, why not the strength to exist? "From that moment on," Rilke writes, "I have known with certainty that the worst things, and even despair, are only a kind of abundance and an onslaught of existence that one decision of the heart could turn into its opposite." I feel the force of that conversion when I read lines of Rilke's, lines with a sudden intensity that seems to burn a hole through the paper of reality: "Whoever has no house now, will never have one. / Whoever is alone will stay alone." "Oh and night: there is night, when a wind full of infinite space / gnaws at our faces." "That is what fate means: to be opposite, / to be opposite and nothing else, forever." Lines that rip the sheet off reality, leaving only the naked ghost.

It had started to become almost ritualized speech, to express one's gratitude, to acknowledge how lucky we were for what we had, to still be alive. And I was lucky, if life is luck—Whitman said dying is lucky. But I could be, when alone, so fiercely protective of my despair. Reading Rilke in the dark seemed to carve out a room, farther inside, where I was allowed to despair, and it made me so happy.

Insane Places

In 1973, the psychologist David Rosenhan published a paper in the journal *Science* called "On Being Sane in Insane Places." The paper was based on an experiment he had conducted, sometimes called "the Thud experiment," designed to interrogate how we distinguish the sane from the insane, if in fact sanity and insanity are distinguishable states. Rosenhan arranged to have eight "pseudopatients" seek voluntary admission to a psychiatric hospital. The instigating complaint was of auditory hallucinations: the patients claimed to hear voices saying the words "empty," "hollow," and "thud." All eight were admitted into psychiatric wards, most with a diagnosis of schizophrenia.

Once in the wards, the patients experienced some initial anxiety—they hadn't expected to get in so easily—but then proceeded to act normally. Rosenhan writes:

> The pseudopatient, very much as a true psychiatric patient, entered a hospital with no foreknowledge of when he would be discharged. Each was told that he would have to get out by his own devices, essentially by convincing the staff that he was sane. The psychological stresses associated with hospitalization were

considerable, and all but one of the pseudopatients desired to be discharged almost immediately after being admitted. They were, therefore, motivated not only to behave sanely, but to be paragons of cooperation.

When asked how they were feeling, the patients all said they felt fine and were no longer hearing any voices. But they continued to be treated as though they were schizophrenic. They were kept in the hospital for an average of nineteen days (one for fifty-two days) and when eventually discharged, it was under the assumption of "remission."

Rosenhan (who was himself one of the pseudopatients) came to the conclusion that "we cannot distinguish the sane from the insane in psychiatric hospitals." You could say that the staff were prone to overdiagnosis, or that the structure of the institution creates a hammer-nail relation between doctor and patient—or you could say that the structure of the institution creates the conditions for insanity. Rosenhan claimed that, in a hospital setting, "the normal are not detectably sane." So were they all mad, as in Wonderland? ("How do you know I'm mad?" said Alice. "You must be," said the Cat, "or you wouldn't have come here.") (It must be noted that the validity of the study, and indeed most studies, has been called into question.)

The surrealist writer and painter Leonora Carrington was once, during World War II, institutionalized against her will. Max Ernst, her partner (if that is the right word—they were living together, though he was married to someone else—Wikipedia uses "lover," which does not sound objective), had been captured by the Nazis. His art was considered degenerate. It seems fair to say she temporarily lost her mind—war is an insane place. Sickened by injustice, she drank orange blossom water to make herself vomit, to purge herself of the "brutal ineptitude of society"; she saw her stomach as "a mirror" of the world. The sequence of events, by her own account, is confusing, but she managed to escape with two friends from France to Madrid and ended up in an asylum in Santander, a town on the northern coast of Spain.

Down Below, written in 1943, is Carrington's brief memoir of this period. The doctor was injecting her with Cardiazol, a drug that induces seizures, for so-called convulsive therapy. Carrington described the occurrence of the first injection as "the most terrible and blackest day in my life"—"How can I write this when I'm afraid to think about it?" (I'm reminded of Plath's first experience with electroshock therapy, which was so physically and psychologically painful for her that she swore to kill herself before undergoing it again.) For ten minutes, Carrington suffered "the Great Epileptic Ailment": "I was convulsed, pitiably hideous, I grimaced and my grimaces were repeated all over my body." Afterward, as some kind of antidote, she asked for lemons and "swallowed them with their rinds." An article on the history of Cardiazol treatment in British mental hospitals, by the researcher Niall McCrae, asks, "What made Cardiazol work—or appear to work?" He suggests that "the intense fear experienced during treatment—the major reason for abandoning Cardiazol in favour of electroshock—was therapeutically advantageous"; that patients, in other words, could be scared sane, which is possibly true. But in the short term, the drug only made Carrington behave more insanely. She became convinced that these "purifying tortures" would help her attain "Absolute Knowledge," which she needed to unite the cosmos and save the world. It seems the treatments for madness quite often have madness as a side effect.

Carrington's biography, a friend informs me, is rife with conflicting and erroneous information—perhaps inevitable for a darling of the surrealist movement. André Breton seemed almost jealous of Carrington's "voyage to the other side of reason," as Marina Warner puts it in her introduction to *Down Below*—as if madness were a career achievement. A version of Carrington's episode in the sanatorium also found its way into one of her novels, *The Hearing Trumpet*, written in the fifties or early sixties. But it's not lightly fictionalized autobiography along the lines of *The Bell Jar*. Here the experience is transformed into something more fabulist, and much more interesting than the memoir. In the novel, delusions of grandeur become real powers.

The Hearing Trumpet's first sentence reveals the inciting incident, or perhaps the inciting object, the magic charm that sets events in motion: "When Carmella gave me the present of the hearing trumpet she may have foreseen some of the consequences." Carmella is Marian Leatherby's prescient, resourceful friend; Marian is a ninety-two-year-old English woman living in Spain with her son Galahad and his family, who, she has noticed, have ceased to find her worthwhile. Because of her deafness, or perhaps just because she is old, they treat her like an insect, or a ghost, as though she were fully insensate or already dead; she enters through the back of the house like a dog. The maid, Rosina, "seems generally opposed to the rest of humanity" and yet they get along: "I do not believe that she puts me in a human category so our relationship is not disagreeable." The

hearing trumpet, "a fine specimen of its kind," "exceptionally pretty, being encrusted with silver and mother o'pearl,"
is a bit of a monkey's paw gift. "Your life will be changed,"
Carmella promises—but not necessarily for the better.

Hearing trumpets, an early, analog form of hearing aid,
can be quite effective, and Marian's is, to a frightful degree:
"What I had always heard as a thin shriek went through
my head like the bellow of an angry bull." Carmella asks
if Marian can hear her: "Indeed I could, it was terrifying."
The impairment had been, in a way, a gift of its own, shield-
ing her from the worst of humanity, and her family's own
cruelty. At Carmella's urging, she uses the instrument to
spy on her family, and overhears them plotting to put her
away. "Your mother has been a constant anxiety to us for
the past twenty years," Muriel, her daughter-in-law, says;
their son Robert is less kind: "She's a drooling sack of de-
composing flesh." They are sure she'll be "better off in a
home," if not "better off dead," and in any case unlikely to
"even notice the change."

Marian lowers the hearing trumpet and concedes, to herself, that she may be senile—"but what does senile mean?"
The institution where they want to send her, Santa Brigada,
run by "the Well of Light Brotherhood," "sounds more terrifying than death itself"—and yet, she has her own ideas
about her right to exist ("I consider that I am still a useful
member of society"). She is not ready to die and in fact her
own mother is still alive, in good health though "getting
old"(!). Marian dreams of going to Lapland, stopping to visit
her mother on the way, then spending the rest of her days
in the snow among "dogs, woolly dogs." She doesn't fight
her family's decision. "Nothing I can say will change your

opinion," she says. "You are right from your own point of
view." She concedes the relativity of reality. Galahad assures
her this is for her own good and that she won't be lonely. "I
am never lonely, Galahad," she replies. "Or rather I never
suffer from loneliness. I suffer much from the idea that my
loneliness might be taken away from me."

Because "one has to be very careful what one takes when
one goes away forever," Marian decides to pack "as if I were
going to Lapland." (In 1940, before leaving Saint-Martin
for Spain, Carrington spent a night "carefully sorting" the
things she would bring along with her. Later, these effects
took on talismanic importance: "My red-and-black refill
pencil [leadless] was Intelligence . . . A box of Tabu pow-
der with a lid, half grey and half black, meant eclipse, complex, vanity, taboo, love.") Marian feels "too preoccupied"
to sleep, but then, "sleeping and waking are not quite as
distinctive as they used to be." Day dreaming and night
dreaming blur into each other, as in the hypnagogic visions,
or near hallucinations, some people see when they're falling asleep (Carrington was among them). The next day,
Galahad and Muriel drive Marian to Santa Brigada, which
is not quite the prison complex that Marian and Carmella
had envisioned, but "a castle, surrounded by various pavil-
ions with incongruous shapes":

> Pixielike dwellings shaped like toadstools, Swiss cha-
> lets, railway carriages, one or two ordinary bungalows,
> something shaped like a boot, another like what I took
> to be an outsize Egyptian mummy. It was all so very
> strange that I for once doubted the accuracy of my
> observation.

That "for once" is perplexing, because Marian frequently calls into question the accuracy of her observations. Not long after she overhears her daughter-in-law say "She doesn't have any idea where she is," which is plainly untrue, she goes into a waking reverie, in her own backyard while, "strangely enough," also in England, "under a lilac bush." She knows she is not in England—"I am inventing all this and it is about to disappear"—still, it is England she sees. She speaks of the "fancies" that keep her amused during "sleepless nights," since "old people do not sleep much." Or is she sleeping and dreaming all the time? Her room at the institution has trompe l'oeil furniture: a "painted wardrobe" on the wall, "an open window with a curtain fluttering in the breeze, or rather it would have fluttered if it were a real curtain." *Real?* All fictive furniture is fake, but this novel has real fake furniture and fake fake furniture. Here the novelist seems to be poking holes and peeking through the text. Sleeping and waking are fluid, as are reality and fiction (or reality and surreality).

Can Marian be trusted? Can Carrington? I've heard it said that "all narrators are unreliable," but the narrator of a memoir is unreliable in a way that the narrator of a novel never is. In *Down Below*, Carrington writes, of her own behavior, "I did not remember any of this." We can't know what happened, we can't distinguish between the sanity and the insanity in Santander. But in Santa Brigada? Despite her age and infirmities, her bouts of imaginative dozing, as the events of *The Hearing Trumpet* get more fantastical, I must believe Marian's version of events is *real*. There can be no other account. What she sees (and hears) in the world of this novel just is what "happens": she's introduced to the

bizarre, cultish logic of the institution's doctrine, "Inner
Christianity"; she meets the other residents (or patients, or
inmates) and gets wind of their underground schemes; she
wonders after the source of a painting of a winking nun, a
"leering abbess," hung across from her place at the dining
table; she is given, by a woman named Christabel Burns,
a tract about the figure, the whole of which appears as a
text within the text (from pages 90 to 126, almost 20 percent of the novel); she witnesses Natacha Gonzalez and Vera
Van Tocht making a poisoned batch of fudge, which Maude
Wilkins mistakenly eats, dying in the process; she climbs a
ladder to peer into Maude's room through a skylight, and
sees the naked corpse of not a woman but a man (cock and
balls helpfully illustrated, in one of a number of drawings by
Carrington's son in the book); she joins the other women,
all but Natacha and Vera and Maude, in a hunger strike,
since eating no longer seems safe. This is survivable only
because Carmella has snuck in some port and chocolate
biscuits, which the ladies ration and share at night, by the
bee pond, where they meet in a sort of witches' sabbath and
trance out in a "weird dance" that seems normal to them at
the time.

As Christabel beats her tom-tom and chants, a cloud
rises from the pond, "an enormous bumble bee as big as a
sheep." Marian reflects: "All this may have been a collective hallucination although nobody has yet explained to me
what a collective hallucination actually means." What dis-
tinguishes hallucination from reality, the fake reality from
the real reality, in a surrealist novel? If we believe anything,
why not believe this? The weather turns cold, quite cold
for Spain—"so cold that hoarfrost glittered over the garden

every morning." The agèd women are underfed and have no fur coats, yet Marian is happy. Because they're not eating, they can no longer be forced to work in the kitchen. Suddenly they are free. The earth's polarity is literally shifting. The sun stops rising; day merges into night; they stop using the word "day." Marian's life has changed, certainly. "The sparkling white frost brought a strange joy into my heart, and I thought about Lapland." Because she could not go to Lapland, Lapland came to her.

On the next-to-last page of *The Hearing Trumpet*, Marian says, "This is the end of my tale. I have set it all down faithfully and without exaggeration either poetic or otherwise." It reminds me of a moment in the 1810 German novella *Michael Kohlhaas*, by Heinrich von Kleist, an aside from the almost invisible narrator, in preface to a strikingly unlikely coincidence: "Just as verisimilitude and fact are not always perfectly aligned, something happened next that we will report, but permit readers who prefer to doubt it to doubt." We *may* doubt it, but would we? And why? I love when a piece of fiction insists that it's true. Inside itself, it always is.

The Uncanny Child

When I was a child, my mother always asked me to set the table before dinner. If there was anything odd among the four place settings—a chipped plate, say, or a knife from a different pattern—I came to believe the person I gave it to would die. My habit in the beginning was to give it to my brother; later, my mother; and later still, my father. I can't explain these decisions. Night after night, no one would die, but my belief in this power, my fear of this power, persisted. By the time I was twelve or thirteen, I'd mostly outgrown the belief. I had talked myself out of other secret, compulsive behaviors, like counting things pointlessly, never stepping on a certain corner tile in the foyer. Still, when setting the table, I began to take the doomed object, the portent, for myself—superstitiously, just in case.

Ellen, the eleven-year-old narrator of Linda Boström Knausgård's novella *Welcome to America*, believes she has similar powers, but life has provided her with more evidence that they're real: "My dad's dead. Did I mention that? It's my fault. I prayed out loud to God for him to die and he did." In the aftermath, Ellen has stopped talking or even writing—communication is dangerous, any crossing of the barrier between inner life and outer world. "You should never ask for what you want," Ellen says, or maybe thinks—the transmission of this confession somehow bypasses her silence:

> It disturbs the order of things. The way you really want them. You want to be disappointed. You want to be hurt and have to struggle to get over it. You want the wrong presents on your birthday.

Ellen does not feel remorse about her father, whose moods were erratic and threatened of violence; he made her mother and everyone unhappy: "I never felt guilty about wishing he was dead." She reasons it was murder in self-defense, and further, she is not fully responsible, since she achieved the killing through prayer. God is her co-conspirator: "It was me and God who'd killed my dad. We'd done it together, once and for all." But she is afraid of her own power, "the power there was in me speaking." She quickly realizes silence is another kind of power—the power of withholding what other people want ("It was so easy. Just stopping. From one moment to the next my life was changed"). It's a power she must have the strength of will to maintain: "Sometimes I'm scared I'll talk in my sleep. That someone will hear me and hold it against me at some future time." Ellen has spent so much of her childhood in fear—in her silence, finally, she becomes frightening, a threat and not the threatened.

Horror movies are full of silent, glaring children—the demonic little blondes in *Village of the Damned*; the twins at the end of the hallway in *The Shining*; tiny telekinetic Drew

Barrymore in *Firestarter*. Part of the creep factor of the silent child is that we don't know what they're thinking. Are they judging us? Scheming? A truly silent child stares like a doll. In his definitive essay on the uncanny, Sigmund Freud mentions a woman patient who "even at the age of eight" was still convinced that "her dolls would be certain to come to life if she were to look at them in a particular way, with as concentrated a gaze as possible." What's uncanny about a living doll or a doll-like child is not the realization of a childhood fear, Freud argues—"the child had no fear of its doll coming to life, it may even have desired it." Rather the doll reminds us of "an infantile wish," the wish to make something true just by thinking it—desire as a power in itself.

Freud goes on to tell an anecdote about another patient who had an excellent stay in a spa owing mostly to his room, "which immediately adjoined that of a very amiable nurse." When he returned to the establishment,

> he asked for the same room but was told that it was already occupied by an old gentleman, whereupon he gave vent to his annoyance in the words "Well, I hope he'll have a stroke and die." A fortnight later the old gentleman really did have a stroke. My patient thought this an "uncanny" experience.

Freud calls this type of experience "omnipotence of thoughts," a "narcissistic overestimation" of the influence of our desires. Irrational narcissism is natural in children, but we unlearn it in adulthood. When a flash of it returns, there's recognition. The uncanny, for Freud, is the eerily familiar, "something familiar and old . . . estranged only by the process of repression."

In *The Disappearance of Childhood*, Neil Postman argues that the construct of adulthood is based partially on shame. Children, he writes, "are immersed in a world of secrets, surrounded by mystery and awe." Adults make the world intelligible to children by teaching them "how shame is transformed into a set of moral directives." Adults know the rules, what can and cannot be said, what words and acts are shameful. "From the child's point of view, shame gives power and authority to adulthood." According to Postman, the gap between childhood and adulthood was a side effect of literacy. In the Middle Ages, childhood ended at seven "because that is the age at which children have command over speech." The chasm widened in the age of print because there was so much more to learn: "A new kind of adulthood had been invented. From print onward, adulthood had to be earned."

Boström Knausgård's Ellen knows on some level that speaking and writing are connected to a transformation she resists. She doesn't want to grow up. "I stopped talking when growing began to take up too much space inside me," she thinks. Among the tallest in her class, she can't control her growth spurts the way she can control her speech: "I couldn't refuse food. My hunger was too great." Growing up is *noisy*—her mother, a stage actress, teaches pupils how to scream in their living room; her older brother physically nails his door shut to play guitar with an amp and a drum machine—but childhood is quiet. In her silence she longs to go back, to go backward—a version of repetition-compulsion. "Was I trying to relive my child-hood," she asks, "only this time without dad?"

The *unheimlich* (unhomelike) is tied up with nostalgia—the ache to return home. Ellen rarely leaves their home, though it hardly seems safe—her father still haunts it, or perhaps still haunts only Ellen. The uncanny child is closer to the membrane of the spirit world. His ghost turns up in her room one night, "sitting in the armchair whistling." He lectures and taunts her. "How could I shut him up?" she thinks. The fish-boning knife she keeps hidden in her room is no help, she knows: "He was already dead." Her only recourse is to write in the notebook that is otherwise verboten: *"You're dead. You can't come here."* She gives him the notebook and watches him read. That does the trick. "Printing links the present with forever," Postman writes. "It carries personal identity into realms unknown." Writing makes thoughts more real; it creates reality, turns thoughts into acts.

The thought that one day she "might speak again" is horrible to Ellen, and yet she knows her will has limits. "This staying silent couldn't possibly last a lifetime . . . No one could ask that of me." The only logical, "possible outcome" of her silence is death, she decides, her own death, in youth: "The thought came to me from somewhere that I would have to die." She'll rewind to a time before her existence. She'll undo herself, with God's help—God can still hear her thoughts, and she is sure he will answer her prayers. But "how long would I have to wait?" Literal death is preferable to the end of childhood; to becoming larger, more conspic-uous, more like her father; to being unable to hide: "The whole idea of growing up felt completely wrong . . . I saw no other way." She avoids mirrors, "not wishing to see what growing was doing"—"afraid the transformation had already begun." In leaving childhood, she becomes monstrous. She is afraid of herself, must hide from herself. She must subvert aging through death.

If books invented childhood, in Postman's view, electricity led to its demise—"the telegraph began the process of making information uncontrollable." The telegraph "altered the kind of information children could have access to, its quality and quantity, its sequence, and the circumstances in which it would be experienced." Television in particular hastened the disappearance of childhood as we know it. Suddenly children had access to everything adults knew, in a format they could instantly grasp. I think of Carol Anne in *Poltergeist* communing with the TV set. (Postman quotes Reginald Damerell: "No child or adult becomes better at watching television by doing more of it. What skills are required are so elemental that we have yet to hear of a television viewing disability.") Suddenly children had answers to questions they hadn't asked. And that TV is real, or at least realistic, is what destroys childhood innocence. "To what extent does the depiction of the world *as it is* undermine a child's belief in adult rationality, in the possibility of an ordered world, in a hopeful future?" Postman asks. What happens when children see adults don't know more than they do? Margaret Mead called it a "crisis of faith."

In fiction, the end of childhood is sometimes depicted as an *unheimlich* moment of self-realization in the simplest sense—the moment a child realizes they *are* a self, a singular consciousness distinct from the world. "It happened" to

Frankie, in *The Member of the Wedding* by Carson McCullers, the summer she was twelve and had "grown so tall that she was almost a big freak." What "happened" is so sudden she cannot understand it. Frankie's brother Jarvis has come home from Alaska and announced he's getting married; this changes everything:

> "The world is certainy a small place," she said.
>
> "What makes you say that?"
>
> "I mean sudden," said Frankie. "The world is certainy a sudden place."
>
> "Well, I don't know," said Berenice. "Sometimes sudden and sometimes slow."
>
> Frankie's eyes were half closed, and to her own ears her voice sounded ragged, far away:
>
> "To me it is sudden."

The idea of the wedding gives Frankie "a feeling she could not name." "They were the two prettiest people I ever saw," she says. "I just can't understand how it happened." Jarvis and his bride-to-be are receding from her, through the portal of "the wedding at Winter Hill," into a charmed adult life ("I bet they have a good time every minute of the day") while she is stuck in limbo: "Frankie was too tall this summer to walk beneath the arbor as she had always done before . . . Standing beside the arbor, with dark coming on, Frankie was afraid." She tells Berenice, "I wish I was somebody else except me." Once you know you are a person, you also know you are not, *cannot be*, anyone else. Other people's happiness does not happen to you.

In Richard Hughes's *A High Wind in Jamaica*, a group

of children are captured by pirates. Life on this pirate ship is surprisingly uneventful: "The weeks passed in aimless wandering . . . Things ceased happening." Until, that is, "an event did occur, to Emily, of considerable importance." Emily, who is ten, "suddenly realized who she was." While playing house in a nook near the bow of the ship, "it suddenly flashed into her mind that she was *she*."

She began to laugh, rather mockingly. "Well!" she thought, in effect: "Fancy *you*, of all people, going and getting caught like this!—You can't get out of it now, not for a very long time: you'll have to go through with being a child, and growing up, and getting old, before you'll be quit of this mad prank!"

Then Emily begins to wonder why she is her and not someone else, "out of all the people in the world who she might have been"—"Had she chosen herself, or had God done it?" Was the self a conspiracy with God? Is *she* a god? The "whole fabric" of life, now that she was "discrete," a person with the treacherous power of consciousness, seemed "vaguely disquieting." I had a similar moment in my life, at some point in adolescence. I don't recall the trigger—just where I was, in my bedroom, facing my bookshelves, and a chilling apprehension of myself as a being with an edge, which I was inside. Uncanny.

Writing in 1982, Postman describes the emergence of "an adult-child": "a grown-up whose intellectual and emotional capacities are unrealized and, in particular, not significantly different from those associated with children." Ellen could be a "child-adult," a child whose intellectual and emotional capacities are not significantly different from those of the grown-ups around her. In life, her father was as impetuous and unreliable as a child, and after his death, everyone in Ellen's family believes that someone else is in control: "I thought about who actually decided things in our house and ended up realizing that we all probably thought it was someone else." It's a delicate system of projected responsibility to which "everyone needed to contribute, otherwise it fell apart."

We learn this from Ellen herself of course, first-person, present-tense Ellen: "It was as if the calm that sometimes descended on us was dependent on such a fine-grained network of understanding and good will that no one felt inclined to break with the implicit order of things." At moments like these, Ellen does not sound like a child. I wondered at times if this was sloppiness on behalf of the author or translator, but it could also be intentional, a way of showing that Ellen really is becoming monstrously adult-like, operating with the intellect not of an innocent but a latently criminal mind. "Through the miracle of symbols and electricity our own children know everything any-one else knows—the good with the bad," Postman writes. "Nothing is mysterious, nothing awesome, nothing is held back from public view." There is no shame.

Welcome to America is almost a horror novel; it arouses "dread and creeping horror," as Freud writes of the uncanny, and "all that is terrible." That fileting knife in Ellen's desk drawer is like Alfred Hitchcock's bomb under the breakfast table, a machine of suspense. Ellen's mother's willful denial ("Nothing wrong with us"), her brother's almost flirtatious hints at violence ("Do you want me to hit her?" he asks their mother)—over 124 pages, there's a ratcheting of tension that feels unsustainable. The reader becomes convinced *something* terrible will happen. But what? A rape? More "murder"?

Nothing happens. Ellen tries her mother's cigarettes; her mother is unimpressed, offers her coffee. The child smokes and reads comics on the balcony. "It occurred to me that I might be happy," Ellen thinks. Nevertheless, she expects an early death; she continues to conspire with God, "who was going to cut my life short." The sense of threat, the threat of threat, is never resolved—is that then horror? If the question the fear asks is never answered? In *The Weird and the Eerie*, Mark Fisher writes, "The sensation of the eerie occurs either when there is something present where there should be nothing, or there is nothing present where there should be something." Hence, *an eerie silence*—when you expected a Wilhelm scream.

Though readying for death, Ellen "could not" imagine her family at her funeral. Whether she tries and is unable or simply refuses to indulge in that fantasy isn't clear. Either way, she knows she won't be there. This is how the end of childhood prefigures death. At some undefined moment you cross over; you leave your child self behind. You can't even say goodbye—you won't be there.

Somethingness (or, Why Write?)

I encountered Joan Didion's famous line about why she writes—"entirely to find out what I'm thinking"—many times before I read the essay it comes from, and was reminded once again to never assume you know what anything means out of context. I had always thought the line was about her essays, about writing nonfiction to discover her own beliefs—because of course the act of making an argument clear on the page brings clarity to the writer too. She may have believed that; she may have thought it a truth too obvious to state. In any case, it's not what she meant. She was talking about why she writes *fiction*:

> I write entirely to find out what I'm thinking, what I'm looking at, what I see and what it means . . . Why did the oil refineries around Carquinez Strait seem sinister to me in the summer of 1956? Why have the night lights in the Bevatron burned in my mind for twenty years? *What is going on in these pictures in my mind?*

These pictures, Didion writes, are "images that shimmer around the edges," reminiscent of "an illustration in every elementary psychology book showing a cat drawn by a patient in varying stages of schizophrenia." (I know these frightening psychedelic cats, the art of Louis Wain, very well—I saw them as a child, in just such a book, which I found on my parents' shelves.) *Play It as It Lays*, she explains, began "with no notion of 'character' or 'plot' or even 'incident,'" but with pictures. One was of a woman in a short white dress walking through a casino to make a phone call; this woman became Maria. The Bevatron (a particle accelerator at Berkeley National Lab) was one of the pictures in her mind when she began writing *A Book of Common Prayer*. Fiction, for Didion, was the task of finding "the grammar in the picture," the corresponding language: "The arrangement of the words matters, and the arrangement you want can be found in the picture in your mind. The picture dictates the arrangement." This is a much stranger reason to write than to clarify an argument. It makes me think of the scenes that I sometimes see just before I fall asleep. I know I'm still awake—they're not as immersive as dreams—but they seem to be something that's happening to me, not something I'm creating. I'm not manning the projector.

Nabokov spoke of shimmers too. "Literature was born on the day when a boy came crying wolf, wolf and there was no wolf behind him," he said in a lecture in 1948. "Between the wolf in the tall grass and the wolf in the tall story there is a shimmering go-between." In this view, it seems to me, the writer's not the wraith who can pass between realms of reality and fantasy. The art itself is the wraith, which the artist only grasps at. Elsewhere, Nabokov writes that inspiration comes in the form of "a prefatory glow, not unlike some benign variety of the aura before an epileptic attack."

In his *Paris Review* interview, Martin Amis describes the urge to write this way: "What happens is what Nabokov described as a throb. A throb or a glimmer, an act of recognition on the writer's part. At this stage the writer thinks, Here is something I can write a novel about." Amis also saw images, a sudden person in a setting, as if a pawn had popped into existence on a board: "With *Money*, for example, I had an idea of a big fat guy in New York, trying to make a film. That was all." Likewise for Don DeLillo: "The scene comes first, an idea of a character in a place. It's visual, it's Technicolor—something I see in a vague way. Then sentence by sentence into the breach." For these writers that begin from something like hallucination, the novel is a universe that justifies the image, a replica of Vegas to be built out of words.

William Faulkner wrote *The Sound and the Fury* five separate times, "trying to tell the story, to rid myself of the dream." "It began with a mental picture," he told Jean Stein in 1956, "of the muddy seat of a little girl's drawers in a pear tree." He couldn't seem to get it right, to find the picture's grammar, or hear it. (According to Didion, "It tells you. You don't tell it.") This was part of the work, this getting it wrong—Faulkner believed failure was what kept writers going, and that if you ever could write something equal to your vision, you'd kill yourself. In his own *Paris Review* interview, Ted Hughes tells a story about Thomas Hardy's vision of a novel—"all the characters, many episodes, even some dialogue—the one ultimate novel that he absolutely had to write"—which came to him up in an apple tree. This may be apocryphal, but I hope it isn't. (I imagine him on a ladder, my filigree on the myth.) By the time he came down "the whole vision had fled," Hughes said, like an untold dream. We have to write while the image is shimmering.

There is often something compulsive about the act of writing, as if to cast out invasive thoughts. Kafka said, "God doesn't want me to write, but I must write." Hughes wondered if poetry might be "a revealing of something that the writer doesn't actually want to say but desperately needs to communicate, to be delivered of." It's the fear of discovery, then, that makes poems poetic, a way of telling riddles in the confession booth. "The writer daren't actually put it into words, so it leaks out obliquely," Hughes said. Speaking of Sylvia Plath, in 1995, he added, "You can't overestimate her compulsion to write like that. She had to write those things—even against her most vital interests. She died before she knew what *The Bell Jar* and the *Ariel* poems were going to do to her life, but she had to get them out." Jean Rhys also looked at writing as a purgative process: "I would write to forget, to get rid of sad moments." Some reach a point where the writing is almost involuntary. The novelist Patrick Cottrell has said he writes only when he absolutely has to. "I have to feel borderline desperate," he said, and "going long periods without writing" helps feed the desperation. Ann Patchett, in an essay called "Writing and a Life Lived Well," writes that working on a novel is like living a double life, "my own and the one I create." It's much easier not to be working on a novel—I sometimes hear novelists speak of a work in progress as an all-consuming crisis. But the ease of not working, after a while, feels cheap. Patchett writes, "This life lived only for myself takes on a certain lightness that I find almost unbearable."

Some writers write in the name of Art in general—James

Salter for instance: "A great book may be an accident, but a good one is a possibility, and it is thinking of that that one writes. In short, to achieve." Eudora Welty said she wrote "for *it*, for the pleasure of *it*." Or as Joy Williams puts it, in a wonderfully strange essay called "Uncanny the Singing That Comes from Certain Husks," "The writer doesn't write for the reader. He doesn't write for himself, either. He writes to serve . . . something. Somethingness. The somethingness that is sheltered by the wings of nothingness—those exquisite, enveloping, protecting wings." Is that somethingness the wraith, the shimmering go-between? Or a godlike observer? "The writer writes to serve," she writes, "that great cold elemental grace which knows us."

Though Faulkner felt a duty toward the work that superseded all other ethics ("If a writer has to rob his mother, he will not hesitate; the 'Ode on a Grecian Urn' is worth any number of old ladies"!), he also found writing fun, at least when it was new. David Foster Wallace, in a piece from the 1998 anthology *Why I Write*, edited by Will Blythe, agrees: "In the beginning, when you first start out trying to write fiction, the whole endeavor's about fun . . . You're writing almost wholly to get yourself off." (He's not the only writer in the volume to describe writing as sexual pleasure; William Vollmann claims he would write just for thrills but also likes getting paid, "like a good prostitute.") But once you've been published the innocent pleasure is tainted. "The motive of pure personal fun starts to get supplanted by the motive of being liked," Wallace writes, and the fun "is offset by a terrible fear of rejection." Beyond the pleasure in itself, the fun for fun's sake, writing for fun wards off ego and blinding vanity.

For every author who finds writing fun there is one for whom it's pain, for whom Nabokov's shimmerings would not be benign, but premonitions of the suffering. Ha Jin said, "To write is to suffer." Spalding Gray said, "Writing is like a disease." Truman Capote, in his introduction to *The Collected Works of Jane Bowles*, and perhaps a particularly self-pitying mood, called writing "the hardest work around." Annie Dillard said that "writing sentences is difficult whatever their subject"—and further, "It is no less difficult to write sentences in a recipe than sentences in *Moby-Dick*. So you might as well write *Moby-Dick*." (Annie Dillard says such preposterous things—"Some people eat cars"!) It's fashionable now to object on principle to the idea that writing is hard. Writing isn't hard, this camp says; working in coal mines is hard. Having a baby is hard. But this is a category error. Writing isn't hard the way physical labor or recovery from surgery is hard; it's hard the way math or physics is hard, the way chess is hard. What's hard about art is getting any good, and then getting better. What's hard is solving problems with infinite solutions and your finite brain.

Then there's the question of whether the pain comes from writing or the writing comes from pain. "I've never written when I was happy," Jean Rhys said. "I didn't want to . . . When I think about it, if I had to choose, I'd rather be happy than write." Bud Smith has said he's only prolific because he ditched all his other hobbies, so all he can do is write—but "people are probably better off with a yard, a couple kids, and sixteen dogs." Here's Williams again: "Writing has never given me any pleasure." And then there's Dorothy Parker, simply: "I hate writing." I love writing, but

I hate almost everything about being a writer. The striving, the pitching, the longueurs and bureaucracy of publishing, the professional jealousy, the waiting and waiting and waiting for something to happen that might make it all feel worth it. But when I'm actually writing, I'm happy.

Didion borrowed the title of her lecture "Why I Write" from George Orwell, who in his essay of this name outlined four potential reasons why anyone might write: "Sheer egoism" (Gertrude Stein claimed she wrote "for praise," like Wallace in his weaker moments); "aesthetic enthusiasm" or the mere love of beauty (William Gass: "The poet, every artist, is a maker, a maker whose aim is to make something supremely worthwhile, to make something inherently valuable in itself"); "historical impulse," or "desire to see things as they are, to find out true facts and store them up for the use of posterity"; and finally "political purpose." This last cause was what mattered to Orwell. "Every line of serious work that I have written since 1936"—he was writing this ten years later—"has been written, directly or indirectly, *against* totalitarianism and *for* democratic socialism, as I understand it." He considered it "nonsense, in a period like our own, to think that one can avoid writing of such subjects."

I'm unsure if Orwell meant that avoiding moral subjects was an unthinkable error, or a true impossibility, in the sense that one can't escape the spirit of the age. Was any postwar novel, any novel written or even read in 1946, a war novel ineluctably? Kazuo Ishiguro has said he never writes to assert a moral: "I like to highlight some aspect of being human. I'm not really trying to say, so don't do this, or do that. I'm saying, this is how it feels to me." But having a moral, a didactic lesson, and being moral are different.

Writers might try to avoid an argument and fail, even if it is less a thesis than an emergent property, a slow meaning that arises through cause and effect or mere juxtaposition. Ishiguro's novels, in the course of unfolding, do triangulate a worldview. John Gardner would say, if the work is didactic, that means it's too simple: "The didactic writer is anything but moral because he is always simplifying the argument." (He also said, hilariously, "If you believe that life is fundamentally a volcano full of baby skulls, you've got two main choices as an artist: You can either stare into the volcano and count the skulls for the thousandth time and tell everybody, There are the skulls; that's your baby, Mrs. Miller. Or you can try to build walls so that fewer baby skulls go in.") The book can also stand in as an argument for its own existence. Toni Morrison wrote her first novel to fill what she saw as a treacherous gap in literature, to create a kind of book that she had always wanted to read but couldn't find—a book about "those most vulnerable, most undescribed, not taken seriously little black girls." Her ambition was not to make white people empathize with black girls. "I'm writing for black people," Morrison once said, "in the same way that Tolstoy was not writing for me."

Only one writer in the Blythe anthology, a magazine writer named Mark Jacobson, claims he does it "for the money." ("What other reason could there be? For my soul? Gimme a break.") No one in the book claims they do it for fame, though the luster of fame is tempting, distracting. In a TV documentary about Madonna that I saw many years ago, she said she always knew she wanted to be famous, and didn't really care how she got there—music was just the path that worked out. This is not so different from Susan

Sontag, who was also obsessed with fame from an early age. Plath too made such confessions in her diary. Capote often said he always knew he would be rich and famous. I think the wish for fame is reasonable, since practically there's not much money in writing unless you are famous. For most the rewards are meager. As Salter writes, "So much praise is given to insignificant things that there is hardly any sense in striving for it." The thing about success, good fortune, and maybe even happiness is this: you can see that there are people who "deserve" whatever you have as much as you do, but have less, as well as people who "deserve" it less or equally, and have more. So, at the same time, you want more and feel you don't deserve what you have. It's a source of anxiety, guilt, and resentment, and troubles the very idea of what one "deserves." In the end I believe you don't deserve anything; you get what you get.

I've been collecting these theories of why writers write because so many writers have written about it. I love reading writers on writing. I love writers on their bullshit. During the first year of the pandemic, I developed an addiction to interview podcasts. I started taking very long walks, in part because I had the time, in part so I had something to do while I listened. At first this practice was strategic. I had a book coming out, and I thought of the interviews as training; I thought they would help me get better at talking about my own book. But I was also lonely. I wasn't going to readings or parties, and I missed writers' voices. The practice has diminishing comforts. After a while most writers sound the same, and some days, after bingeing on writers, I can start to feel pointless, redundant. Faulkner said he disliked giving interviews because *he* was "of no importance":

"If I had not existed, someone else would have written me, Hemingway, Dostoyevsky, all of us." (And yet he named himself as one of the five most important authors of the twentieth century; there are limits to humility.) Some days I think the very question is banal, like photos of a writer's "workspace." They're all just desks! Why write? Why do anything? Why *not* write? It's the same as the impulse to make a handprint in wet concrete or trace your finger in the mist on a window. What you wrote, as a kid, on a window was the simplest version of the vision. Why not unburden yourself of the vision? (But why that vision? Why that vision, and why you?)

Tillie Olsen, in her 1965 essay "Silences," called the not-writing that has to happen sometimes—"what Keats called *agonie ennuyeuse* (the tedious agony)"—instead "natural silences," or "necessary time for renewal, lying fallow, gestation." Breaks or blocks, times when the author has nothing to say or can only repeat themselves, are the opposite of "the unnatural thwarting of what struggles to come into being, but cannot." The *un*natural silence of writers is suppression of the glimmer. This is Melville who, in Olsen's words, was "damned by dollars into a Customs House job; to have only occasional weary evenings and Sundays left for writing." And likewise Hardy, who stopped writing novels after "the Victorian vileness to his *Jude the Obscure*," Olsen writes, though he lived another thirty years—thirty years gone, gone as that novel in the apple tree. She quotes a line from his poem "The Missed Train": "Less and less shrink the visions then vast in me." And this same fate came to Olsen herself, who wrote what she wrote in "snatches of time" between jobs and motherhood, until "there came a time when this triple life was no longer possible. The fifteen hours of daily realities became too much distraction for the writing." I read Olsen's essay during a period in my life when stress from my day job, among other sources, was making it especially difficult to write. I didn't have the energy to do both jobs well, but I couldn't choose between them, so I did both badly. Like Olsen, I'd lost "craziness of endurance."

James Thurber said that "the characteristic fear of the American writer" is aging—we fear we'll get old and die or simply lose the mental capacity to do the work we want to do, to make our little bids for immortality. Of late I've been obsessed with the idea of a "body of work." I've gotten it into my head that seven books, even short, minor books, will constitute a body of work, my body of work. When I finish, if I finish, seven books I can retire from writing, or die. But how long can the corpus really outlast the corpse? I heard Nicholson Baker on a podcast say his grandfather, or maybe some uncle or other, was a well-known writer in his day and is now totally unknown. Unless we're very, very famous, we'll be forgotten that quickly, he said, so you might as well write what you want. I think about that a lot. Since I don't have children, I have more time to write than Tillie Olsen did. But I don't have that built-in generation of buffer between my death and obscurity. At least I won't be around to know I'm not known. DeLillo again: "We die indoors, and alone."

For a while I walked so much while listening to writers that I wore clean holes through my shoes. I kept asking myself why I write—or more so, why my default state is writing, since on any given day I might be writing for morality, Art, or attention, for just a little money. It's not as easy or as fun as it used to be, so why do I *keep* writing? (I can't go very long without writing, though I can go for a while without writing something good.) I think I write to think—not to find out what I think; surely I know what I already think—but to do better thinking. Staring at my laptop screen makes me better at thinking. Even thinking about writing makes me better at thinking. And when I'm thinking well, I can sometimes write that rare, rare sentence or paragraph that feels exactly right, only in the sense that I found the exact right sequence of words and punctuation to express my own thought—the grammar in the thought. That rightness feels so good, like sinking an unlikely shot in pool. The ball is away and apart from you, but you feel it in your body, the knowledge of causation. Never mind luck or skill or free will, you caused that effect—you're alive!

Nostalgia for a Less Innocent Time

An aspect of research I do not enjoy is finding out that everything I thought I knew about a subject was wrong. For years I carried a belief in my head that the term "yacht rock" derives from the cover of Crosby, Stills & Nash's 1977 album *CSN*, which features a photograph of David Crosby, Stephen Stills, and Graham Nash—in that order, no less—chilling on a sailboat. If I can believe the internet, this isn't the case—the term did not exist until 2005 and was coined by J. D. Ryznar, Hunter D. Stair, and Lane Farnham, the creators of a mockumentary web series about the musical genre that was known in its own time, the late 1970s and early '80s, as "the West Coast Sound" or "adult-oriented rock." According to these fellows, mockumentarists turned podcasters, and their acolytes, yacht rock—a derogatory category that, like "dad jokes," we've decided to embrace, because liking things we used to mock is bizarrely exhilarating—is not an umbrella term for any song "about a boat, or the ocean, or sailing." Timothy Malcolm, a food editor with strong feelings on this topic, writes that yacht rock "can be characterized as smooth and melodic, and typically combines elements of jazz, rhythm and blues, and rock," with "very little acoustic guitar" but lots of "Fender Rhodes electric piano." The "folkie songs" of Crosby, Stills & Nash, he adds, decidedly do not qualify.

This is too bad, because when I choose a yacht rock station on a streaming music service, the first song I want to hear is never the inevitable first song, which is "Sailing" by Christopher Cross. What I want to hear is "Southern Cross" by Crosby, Stills & Nash. There's a video on You-Tube, which I've watched many dozens of times, of the trio playing this song live at a concert in 1982. It was still pretty much their heyday—the album they were touring, *Daylight Again*, went platinum—but what I love about the video is that they already look washed-up. I am inordinately fond of these middle-aged men in their various stages of balding, overweight, and just unfashionable. Despite the acoustic guitars, the song displays many defining aspects of yacht rock: it's "bubbly" and melodic, "yet oddly complex and intellectual," to use Malcolm's words. The yacht has to bear a lot of metaphorical weight: "I have my ship and all her flags are a flyin' / She is all I have left and music is her name." Stills wrote the lyrics, he explained in the liner notes to the *CSN* box set, "about a long boat trip I took after my divorce . . . It's about using the power of the universe to heal your wounds." The themes of "reassuringly vague escapism" and "heartbroken, foolish men," sailing away from their problems, as various music journalists describe the genre, are also key features—the first episode of *Yacht Rock* is about the writing of the song "What a Fool Believes" by the Doobie Brothers.

There's a scene in the 1984 action/romance movie *Romancing the Stone* where Michael Douglas and Kathleen

Turner take shelter in a wrecked cargo plane in the jungles of Colombia. The plane was transporting weed, a kilo of which he proceeds to throw into the campfire. Stoned, they get to chatting, while the Douglas character ("Jack T. Colton") idly flips through an old issue of *Rolling Stone* he finds in the plane. He sits up and cries out, "Aw, goddamn it man, the Doobie Brothers broke up." (I found this line *hilarious* as a child, though I could not possibly have understood almost anything about it—who the Doobie Brothers were, when they broke up, what "doobie" means or the effects of marijuana—I think we must appreciate the formal properties of jokes before we understand their content.) I bring this up because the movie ends with Jack buying a boat—paid for by selling the giant emerald that was eaten by an alligator they had confronted in Cartagena—so they can literally sail away together. The fantasy of boat life was fundamental to the yuppie dreams of the eighties, and at least as important as the fantasy of sailing itself was the fantasy of being able to afford a boat.

Yacht rock, at its tail end, aged into yuppie rock, alternatively known in my own mind as suit rock: think Huey Lewis, Robert Palmer, and, of course, Phil Collins. In the early days of Genesis, he was post-hippie prog rock, photographed in fleece-lined jackets or shirtless and in cutoffs, with long hair and a surprisingly lush beard, but at the time of my first exposure to Collins, when I was beginning to form memories and an identity, around 1984 or '85, he was always in a suit. He wears a suit—an abstract-print jacket over a white shirt, fully buttoned but without a tie—in the video for "Against All Odds (Take a Look at Me Now)," my sentimental favorite Phil Collins song. In his memoir, *Not*

Dead Yet, he says he wrote most of the song back in 1979, around the same time as "In the Air Tonight," but he didn't finish it until the director Taylor Hackford asked him for a song for the soundtrack to his 1984 movie *Against All Odds* (which is kind of a good movie, worth watching if for no other reason than seeing Jeff Bridges at peak hotness, playing an ex–pro football player). He wears a suit—a double-breasted tan suit, with a yellow tie—in the video for "Easy Lover," his duet with Philip Bailey from Earth, Wind & Fire, a song that in the past few years has begun to follow me everywhere; I seem to hear it on car radios or over the PA system in grocery stores about once a week. (I'm not complaining.) He wears a suit—gray, double-breasted, yellow tie, white sneakers—in the video for "Sussudio," a non-sense word that Collins says came "out of nowhere." "I can't think of a better word that scans as well as 'sussudio,' so I keep it and work around it," he says in his (ghostwritten) memoir. This makes no sense at all, since what he actually sings is "susussudio," with an extra syllable. "If I could have a pound for every time I've been asked what the word means," Collins says, "I'd have a lot of pounds" (doesn't he?). (The whole memoir, for some reason, is written in the present tense, so you get sentences like "Things are bad at home—his wife Jill is having a difficult pregnancy, which is not something I'm aware of at the time.") He's wearing a suit in the video for "One More Night"—the video is black-and-white, so it's hard to say exactly what color the suit is, but even in gray scale it looks like his signature yellow tie. He's wearing a suit in the video for "Two Hearts"—actually several different suits, since he plays every player in his band in the video. He wears a suit—gray sleeves pushed up to the elbow—in a Michelob commercial from 1986 that is almost a video for the Genesis song "Tonight, Tonight, Tonight." This commercial, a montage of concert footage and steamy yuppie nightlife in what I took to be downtown Manhattan, informed my whole idea of adulthood. (I never noticed, but apparently the song is about drug addiction, so using it to sell beer is kind of like playing "Pink Houses" at the Republican National Convention.)

I honestly love this era of Phil Collins. George Bradt, a research analyst at MTV from 1983 to 1988, has said, "The best 'testing' artist of all was probably Phil Collins. Research showed that viewers never got tired of his videos, so they were played regularly, months or even years after they were hits." He was writing and recording both with Genesis and as a solo artist, doing production work or drumming for people like Eric Clapton and Robert Plant (whom he calls "Planty"), and appearing on benefit singles like "Do They Know It's Christmas?" and in benefit concerts like Live Aid. He was ubiquitous, and now he has a kind of sheepish defensiveness about his success, like *Could I help it if I couldn't stop writing gold hits?* At one point in *Not Dead Yet*, he says that *No Jacket Required* sold twenty-five million copies—"I only know this because I looked it up on Wikipedia"! "In the eye of the tornado" he couldn't be bothered to keep up with his sales. It was a baffling choice for the name of his '85 album, considering his penchant for jackets. The story is that he and Planty were trying to get a drink at a hotel bar in Chicago, but they wouldn't let him in without a jacket. "I am wearing a jacket," Collins said. "A proper jacket, sir . . . Not leather," the man replied. "I've always hated stuffiness and snobbery," Collins writes, "so *No Jacket*

Required becomes my album title and, yes, why not, ethos." Collins's album titles are uniquely terrible—why so many ellipses? He titled his first hits album . . . *Hits.*

Phil Collins's discography is fascinating because his good songs are *so* good and his bad songs are *so* bad. I truly hate "A Groovy Kind of Love," a cover song from 1988—it is unlistenably bad, much more offensive than the original version, recorded by the Mindbenders, a beat rock group, in 1965. Collins slows it down to the syrupy tempo of a music box lullaby. "Another Day in Paradise" is down at the bottom with it. From his 1989 album . . . *But Seriously,* the single was a number-one hit and won a Grammy for Record of the Year. It's odd because I think of it as a song that everyone always despised. (It stands to reason that the more popular something is, the more well-known it is, the more people have the opportunity to hate it: the Eagles' *Greatest Hits* effect.) I remember reading an article in *Sassy* magazine in the early nineties in which a male, possibly British staffer made fun of Collins's worrying over the homeless problem, writing something very close to, "Maybe it's because you have all the money, ya bald bastard." Collins's yuppie era had given us tracks like "Take Me Home," one of the good ones, a pop song that fits right in with hair metal's odes to road fatigue. "I've been a prisoner all my life," Collins sings, which makes me think of Lady Gaga tweeting, "Fame is prison." The video shows him traveling the world—lip-synching in front of international destinations from the Eiffel Tower to the Sydney Opera House to the Hollywood sign. But the eighties were almost over, and people were starting to tire of yuppie excess. Some of them, at least, were also starting to tire of Phil Collins. His management supposedly called MTV and asked them to play his videos less.

"I'm loath to use the dreaded eighties phrase 'conscience rock,'" Collins says, but he wasn't so loath to write conscience rock. He got the idea for "Another Day in Paradise" during the tour for *Invisible Touch*. When the band landed in DC, Collins asked their driver about "the cardboard boxes lined along the pavements in the shadow of the Capitol Building." He was "gobsmacked" to learn they were "the homes of the homeless"—"so many of them, so close to all this wealth and power." *Dude*, one can't help but think. The song was seen as exploitative by many, just clueless and cringey by others. I'm not entirely sure why the Genesis song "Land of Confusion," which also has a "message," feels less cheesy and detestable—maybe because it's more upbeat, with a sort of funny video (featuring life-size puppets of Ronald and Nancy Reagan). Its politics are also vaguer, a general less-war, more-peace vibe: "There's too many men, too many people . . . And not much love to go round." It's a reminder for the youth that good politics are much more aligned with age cohorts than generations. Mike Rutherford, who wrote the lyrics, was born in 1950. Collins, who sings them, was born in 1951. The song makes the claim that their own generation wasn't making empty promises. The video is going for laughs, though—it ends with the Ronald puppet trying to call for his nurse and accidentally hitting the "Nuke" button instead.

"Another Day in Paradise" is comparatively maudlin, maudlin by any standards really. It takes itself utterly seriously. The video begins with a shot of Earth from space, a version of the "Blue Marble" image that famously inspired the environmental movement. (Many astronauts claim that seeing our planet from space completely changed their perspective on global relations, a phenomenon known as the "overview effect.") As we zoom into Earth, the color goes sepia tone: instant melancholy. In between clips of Collins singing with a highly furrowed brow, we see a bunch of still shots of homeless people sleeping in the street, a few stats about homelessness in all-caps text ("3 MILLION HOMELESS IN AMERICA") as if in a PowerPoint presentation. Some of these images are really harrowing—a shirtless child lying on newspaper, a flap of cardboard over his head. Watching the video again as I write this, for the first time in many years, I don't know quite how to feel about it. Because I'm me, of course I think of Sontag, who writes in *Regarding the Pain of Others* that for "antiwar polemicists," "war is generic" and images of war "are of anonymous, generic victims." As such, a photo of a child killed in wartime might be used toward any end, to justify any position: "Alter the caption, and the children's deaths could be used and reused." You can look at all painful images as manipulative, in this light. In Collins's case, a slideshow of the homeless is being used to sell records. He did donate a bunch of money to homeless shelters during this time, though—his intentions weren't terrible. I think I hate the song in part because I can't entirely hate it; my distaste is too close to ambivalence. The piano part is undeniably catchy. It's a song I might catch myself humming along to before, with a jolt, I remember I don't like it and change the station.

Collins's appeals for sympathy in *Not Dead Yet* read as

kind of pathetic, and he knows it. In a passage about his former bandmate Peter Gabriel (Gabriel left Genesis in 1975),
Collins writes:

> I do envy Pete. There are some songs he's written that
> I wish I'd written—for one thing "Don't Give Up," his
> gorgeous duet with Kate Bush. But even here at the
> height of my success it seems that, for every achieve-
> ment or great opportunity that comes my way, I'm
> starting to accrue bad press as a matter of course. Pete
> seems to get good press seemingly equally automati-
> cally. It seems a bit unfair, which I appreciate is a pa-
> thetic word to use in this context. A few years later, in
> 1996, when I release *Dance into the Light*, *Entertainment
> Weekly* will write: "Even Phil Collins must know that
> we all grew weary of Phil Collins."

For Phil Collins to whinge about unfairness is of course
absurd—but he kind of has a point. Critical attention and
favor are whimsical; some great artists are recognized in
their time, while others are not; otherwise Herman Melville
wouldn't have died in near poverty. This is not to say that
Peter Gabriel isn't good, just that it can always be counted
as luck—coincidence, even—when good art is appreciated
in kind. (I too wish I wrote "Don't Give Up," because then
I'd get to be in the video, hugging Kate Bush for six and a
half minutes straight.) Pathetic or not, Collins is a somewhat sympathetic figure, to me. In late life, as he tells it in
the memoir's penultimate chapter, he moved to Switzerland
to be near two of his kids, though he had divorced their
Swiss mother; he became a full-blown alcoholic out of sheer

boredom. He eventually had to be put on Antabuse, which blocks the enzyme that allows your body to metabolize alcohol, so he could stop drinking and not die of pancreatitis. (Duff McKagan, the bassist from Guns N' Roses, almost died this way too—after years of drinking ten bottles of wine a day, an effort to cut back after years of drinking gallons of vodka, his pancreas burst and gave him third-degree burns on his internal organs. In the ER, the morphine they gave him had next to no effect. He begged the doctors to kill him.)

Nothing Collins says in his book is especially insightful. (When I was reading it, or skimming it anyway, I saw a conversation on Twitter about who qualifies as a "writer's writer." I joked that Phil Collins is definitely not that, and at least four or five people replied that he is, however, a "drummer's drummer.") But I'm fond of him, the way I'm fond of fat David Crosby, who sang backing vocals on "Another Day in Paradise." (They sang it together on *The Arsenio Hall Show*! Collins wears a gray suit over a black shirt with an improbably large collar, almost forming its own bow tie; Crosby's mustache, the ideal mustache, maybe the only mustache in history I like, and his muttonchops are nearing full gray.) I'm fond of Collins's hairline, a deep male-pattern-baldness version of a widow's peak, like the grandpa from *The Munsters* but fluffier. I'm fond of his corny dance moves, the little toe-taps and bounces. And I'm fond of his wardrobe, the bucket hats and Hawaiian shirts, the pleated pants, the sweater-vests over polos, and yes, the suits. They remind me of a brief time when it seemed cool to be an adult, and to do adult-signifier things like work on Wall Street and have an accountant. I may not have yearned for a yacht per se, but I couldn't wait to be old enough to wear shoulder pads and "pumps," to go to a franchise fern bar and order something like an Irish coffee. Adulthood meant freedom of choice, and that, to me, was glamour—not sailing but the ability, the option to sail.

I was six or whatever, so I didn't understand that by the time I was old enough to do those things, they wouldn't be cool anymore. I experience this as an actual loss: I never got to have that alternate life as an adult in the eighties. Nostalgia is a kind of pain.

The Decline of Western Civilization Part II: The Metal Years is a documentary that often feels like a mockumentary—in part because of the inherent absurdity of the LA metal scene in the late 1980s, in part because of Penelope Spheeris's directorial choices. Spheeris, of *Wayne's World* fame, let her subjects decide how they wanted to be filmed. Gene Simmons of Kiss did his interview in a lingerie store—"I don't want to do anything tacky," he'd told her. Simmons's bandmate Paul Stanley suggested, "How about in bed with a bunch of women?" His segments were filmed from above, with lingerie models absentmindedly stroking his spandex pants. Chris Holmes, the lead guitarist from W.A.S.P., suggested, "How about drowning in a pool with my mother watching?"

In what is probably the film's best-known scene, Holmes floats in a pool chair, wearing black leather pants, and tells Spheeris he's a "full-blown alcoholic." To prove it, he pours vodka from a liter of Smirnoff down his throat and all over his face for almost ten seconds. His mother, Sandy

Holmes, who has strong June Cleaver vibes, is indeed there watching from the side of the pool, looking disappointed but resigned. He says, "I'm a happy camper." Spheeris asks him if he wishes he was a bigger star. "I wish I was a smaller star," he answers. "I don't dig being the person I am." Later, after we've seen several musicians say that metal is better than sex, Spheeris cuts back to Holmes in the pool making a jerking-off motion and saying, "It's like this, I love it, it's great," with a cigarette hanging out of his mouth. We hear Spheeris off camera: "It's like beating off?" "It's worse than that," he says. (I can't explain why, but I love him.) Simmons, back in the lingerie store, says that anyone who claims "it's lonely at the top" is "full of it": "It's the best." Back to Holmes in the pool: "I would rather be broke and happy than rich and sad." If only we were given that choice.

Most everyone in the film ends up looking ridiculous. Some random scenester tells Spheeris, "I don't work, I can't stand work." She asks, "What was the last job you had?" "Uh," he says, "I've never had a job." Paul Stanley remarks thoughtfully, "Once you have money, you realize that it's really not important." In one of my favorite moments, Spheeris goes to the Cathouse, Riki Rachtman's "big fun sleazy" club a couple of miles south of the Strip (Rachtman later went on to host MTV's *Headbangers Ball*), and asks some people why they go there. The response is just metal word salad: "Fucking rock!" "Heavy metal!" "Party!" "Drink!" "Guns N' Roses!" "LA!" In another notorious scene, Spheeris films Ozzy Osbourne making breakfast in a leopard-print robe; there's a close-up shot of him attempting to pour orange juice in a glass and spilling it all over the counter. Spheeris later admitted in an interview that part was a stunt: "I faked the orange juice spill." But most of the stupid excess was real—or maybe in the metal years, the line between stunt and reality was blurry.

In their tell-all collective memoir *The Dirt*, the members of Mötley Crüe show the extent of the era's depravity in great detail. The bassist Nikki Sixx describes a day on tour when Ozzy Osbourne announced he "fancied a bump," but they'd run out of coke. (Picture broad daylight: "We rolled out of the bus under the heat of the noonday sun and went straight to the bar.") "Unfazed," he crouched down on the sidewalk and snorted a line of live ants. Trying to keep up ("we wanted to maintain our reputation as rock's most cretinous band"), Sixx "whipped out [his] dick in full view of everyone" and pissed on the floor. Ozzy crawled over and licked at the puddle. At that point Sixx had to admit defeat: "From that moment on, we always knew that wherever we were, whatever we were doing, there was someone who was sicker and more disgusting than we were."

And they were profoundly disgusting. When I picked up the book, I looked at the table of contents, figuring I could just skip to the depravity chapter. But every chapter is the depravity chapter, with titles like "Born Too Loose," "Save Our Souls," "Girls, Girls, Girls," "Some of Our Best Friends Are Drug Dealers," and "Some of Our Best Friends Were Drug Dealers." The first paragraph has the word "cum" in it. (It also opens with an epigraph by Wilkie Collins. Their ghostwriter outdid himself.) In the early days, the apartment they shared, which was near the Whisky a Go Go and functioned as a de facto nightly after-party, had alcohol and bloodstains all over the carpets; the walls were scorched black because the band "couldn't afford pesticides" so they torched the roaches with hairspray and a lighter. They also "couldn't afford" toilet paper, so the bathroom was littered with "shit-stained socks." As much as they brag about their substance abuse and sexual exploits, metal dudes also love to brag about how broke they were before they hit it big. In "The Definitive Oral History of '80s Metal," published in *Salon*, Jani Lane of Warrant claims, "We went down to the store every day and got a jar of peanut butter and a loaf of bread and put the peanut butter on the bread using a Social Security card." Because, I guess, they couldn't afford a plastic knife? I hope the card was laminated.

W.A.S.P. was known for throwing raw meat at the audience. There is no why. Wrongness was the point, an amorality unto nonsense. In *The Dirt*, Sixx describes some "ideas" he had for Mötley Crüe's second album, *Shout at the Devil*: "I had grand ideas of creating a tour that looked like a cross between a Nazi rally and a black church service." They did a full photo shoot in Nazi regalia, but their record company drew the line there. It's not that the band held any fascist beliefs per se; they held no beliefs, apart from embracing provocation and "evil" in all forms. Front man Vince Neil once said, "Nobody's really into the devil. It's showmanship." But Sixx seemed to get confused by his own antics, flirting with genuine Satanism for a while, as if it were the only logical end point of the atmosphere of escalating chaos. When he crashed his Porsche into a telephone pole, he interpreted the accident as a sign that maybe he'd been dabbling a bit too much in devil worship. He got into heroin instead. Sixx was once legally dead from an overdose for about two minutes, but woke up, left the hospital, and shot up again. I think of the "Behind the Laughter" episode of *The Simpsons*, a parody of VH1's *Behind the Music*, where Homer says, "Fame was like a drug, but what was even more like a drug was the drugs."

The members of Mötley Crüe were generally encouraged in these directions. "The more fucked up we got, the greater people thought we were," Sixx writes. "Radio stations brought us groupies; management gave us drugs." I won't go so far as to say they were blameless for their "cretinous" behavior—but in a way everyone around them was also to blame. Reading *The Dirt* made me feel guilty—not in the sense of a guilty pleasure, but with actual guilt. (I was alive in the eighties—I watched MTV—I share in the blame.) I got a little nauseous. After reading it for most of the day, I went to a housewarming party, took one sip of white wine and felt already addled, as if I couldn't remember how many drinks I'd had.

Things get weird for the guys when they finally suffer some consequences worse than a hangover. On the fourth night of a debauched celebration to kick off their third album, *Theatre of Pain* (amazingly, it's meant to be an Artaud reference), Vince Neil and Razzle from the Finnish band Hanoi Rocks ran out for more liquor and Neil wrecked the car. "We were both fucked up and shouldn't have driven," Neil writes, "especially since the store was only a couple blocks away and we could have easily walked." Razzle died in the accident. Neil was charged with involuntary manslaughter and eventually sentenced to thirty days in jail and five years of probation. It created a divide between him and the rest of the band, a cloud of resentment and cognitive dissonance. Sixx writes, "When I thought about Vince, it wasn't with pity; it was with anger, as if he was the bad guy and the rest of the band members were innocent victims of his wrongdoing. But we all did drugs and drove drunk. It could have happened to any of us."

Through the fog of vice and perversion, there are occasional hints of remorse and something close to moral clarity—like the part where Sixx remembers a woman he knew grabbing his hand and pulling him, "slurring and stumbling," into a closet at a party. "We fucked for a while," he writes, then he sent Tommy Lee in. The next day she called him, "her voice trembling," and told him, "I got raped last night." "My heart dropped into my stomach, and my body went cold," Sixx writes. But the woman wasn't talking about him or Lee: "I was hitchhiking home from the Hyatt House, and this guy picked me up and raped me in his car." At first, Sixx was relieved, "because it meant I hadn't raped her"—as if rape is only rape if you're accused of it. "But the more I thought about it, the more I realized that I pretty much had," he writes. He almost gets it—there is almost a reckoning—but he moves quickly on: "I was in a zone, and in that zone, consequences did not exist. Besides, I was capable of sinking even lower than that."

It seems fatuous to linger long on the politics of the scene. It's not as though what was happening is troubling merely in hindsight, by today's higher standards. It's disturbing by any standards; it was disturbing at the time. It was a low point for innocence in pop culture, or a high point for nihilism. The counterculture of the sixties may have given us the principles of "sex, drugs, and rock 'n' roll," but at least they believed in peace and love and "freeing one's mind" to reach a higher consciousness. Metal in the eighties was about pure filthy hedonism for its own sake. As Nikki

Sixx sums it up in a VH1 special called "The Fabulous Life of Mötley Crüe," "We fucked the chicks, we shot the drugs, we wrecked the cars." (The show, narrated by Robin Leach, is mostly a celebration of how Mötley Crüe spent all their money—Sixx built a custom pool in the shape of a vagina, while Neil had thirty-two cars and a mud-wrestling pit.) Misogyny was endemic in the music industry, but metal in particular wore its misogyny with pride. They *performed* it. It was used to disguise the paranoia they must have felt about their androgynous costumes, as if the only way they could get away with wearing that much eye makeup was by coupling it with incandescent sexism and homophobia. They take pleasure in violence to demonstrate their high testosterone. In that same VH1 show, Vince Neil announces, "Just 'cause we wear lipstick don't mean we can't kick your ass."

Still, there were women in the scene who wielded their own kinds of power. Legendary groupie Patti Johnsen said meeting the bands was "a huge high." Some just wanted the same right to rock and get obliterated as the men. According to Iris Berry, formerly of bands including the Lame Flames, Ringling Sisters, Pink Sabbath, Leather Mumu, the Bittersweets, the Flesh Eaters, and Honk If Yer Horny, "If you remember the Rainbow clearly, you weren't really there." (I love the names of metal—the lead singer of London called himself Nadir d'Priest.) Two unnamed girls in *The Decline of Western Civilization Part II* claim that sex is their favorite pastime: "Every day. At least three or four times." Vicky Hamilton, who worked as a manager and promoter for bands including Guns N' Roses, Mötley Crüe, and Poison, was a "freakin genius" according to GNR's original drummer Steven Adler. Rachtman once bragged, "Lita Ford puked in my club!" like it was a true honor. In another (great) VH1 show called "When Metal Ruled the World," Tawny Kitaen—the redhead who dances on the hoods of two Jaguars in Whitesnake's "Here I Go Again" video—says of the time, with starry-eyed reverence, "It was magic." Maybe some of these women were brainwashed, I don't really know. I do remember, as a kid, watching the "chicks" in those videos with a sense of real awe, as though the male gaze transmitted superpowers. I couldn't wait to be a teenager, to be cinematically seventeen. Alas, even at seventeen, I never looked the way seventeen looks on TV.

People think of nostalgia as a yearning for "a more innocent time." But I'm nostalgic for a *less* innocent time, or maybe for the way it felt to watch these scenes of decadence from the perspective of childhood innocence. I was a good kid, too, a teacher's-pet type. I obediently ate all my vegetables, while my older brother snuck into the bathroom and spit his out into the shower stall. But I fucking loved hair metal. (The first comment, with thousands of likes, under a YouTube countdown of the top ten best hair bands is "Motley FUCKING Crue baby!!!" This is the simplicity of sentiment I crave.) My first tapes were Bon Jovi, Def Leppard, Poison. My favorite Poison song was "Fallen Angel"—a play on the cliché of the Hollywood hopeful just off a bus from the Midwest. The guys from Poison were the actual bus-hopping wannabes; they formed in Pennsylvania and then moved to Los Angeles in 1983. But the song is about a girl who leaves home with dreams of becoming an actress, then gets chewed up by the machinery of the scene: Welcome to the jungle, sweetie.

In my endless quest for more hair metal documentaries, I found a compilation of clips titled "Vintage Glam/Hair Metal Interviews Collection (3)" (I couldn't locate parts one and two), which includes a snippet of an interview with a band I'd never heard of named Bang Tango. Here's the lead singer, Joe Lesté, waxing on about their first album, *Psycho Café*: "This is only *Psycho Café* . . . We've got umpteen albums to go . . . We're going to continue to make albums and albums and albums . . . like each album is a kid, like we just had a kid. This is *Psycho Café*, this is our kid." He's completely earnest. They must have felt they were on the verge of true rock stardom—what Mötley Crüe, in a section of *The Dirt* called "An Introduction to Cog Theory," terms "the big cog." Cog theory "is an attempt to pull back the curtain of the popular music business and examine the mechanics of success." Artists start on a conveyor belt, and if they release an album and "experience a degree of success," they get "caught in the machinery" of the first cog. Some musicians move up to the second cog, where "they realize that the machinery is stronger" than they are and "there is no way off." Most bands roll around and around on the second cog and eventually get dropped back at the bottom. But a few, like Mötley, make it to the big cog:

> The big cog is a huge grinding gear, and there's nothing artists can do about it if it picks them up. They can stand up and scream, "I hate everyone in the world and you all suck, and if you buy a single record of mine I'll kill you." And all that will happen is more people will run out and buy their records. Trying to get off the cog is futile: It only makes the process hurt more.

Bang Tango certainly never made it to the big cog. I posted that quote about *Psycho Café* on Twitter, and a friend responded with a link to their video "Someone Like You," saying, "This is certainly vintage 80s hair band, but I have heard of exactly zero of their songs." I'd never heard the song either. A 2015 documentary about the band called *Attack of Life* tries to make the case that Bang Tango never made it really big because they were too unique. (The director, Drew Fortier, later joined the band; I don't think it's objective.) To me, "Someone Like You" looks and sounds like an amalgam of the rest of the genre. It's not good, exactly, but I can see that they might easily have been as famous as Cinderella or whatever, or as any of what Twisted Sister's Dee Snider once referred to as "the *W* bands" (Whitesnake, White Lion, Winger, Warrant). So much of history is interchangeable.

Gene Simmons might think fame is the best, but I'm much more interested in the banality of fame, its emptiness. In my favorite hair metal videos, fame is exhausting, lonely, and *boring*. Vince Neil said that he understood why rock stars have such big egos when he first played for a giant stadium crowd: "From the stage, the world is just one faceless, shirtless, obedient mass, as far as the eye can see." The banality of fame is best captured by the tour montage, an especially popular choice to showcase a power ballad. Take Bon Jovi's perfect video for "Wanted Dead or Alive," which has it all, in slow motion—the grainy black-and-white footage of hands holding up lighters and flashing the sign of the horns; the women in the audience screaming and sobbing and lip-synching, one clutching a single drumstick; the band dragging themselves on and off different modes of transportation, gazing contemplatively out the windows of planes and buses; Jon finally collapsing after the show, dripping with sweat, on a sofa backstage. It's exhaustion pornography—exhaustion as a trophy of excess. Mötley Crüe's video for "Home Sweet Home" is similar, with its time-lapse footage of stage sets being assembled and concertgoers milling around outside stadiums like something from *Koyaanisqatsi*. Inside, women are diving onto the stage and being dragged off by security. But they all still look like they're having a great time—"Home Sweet Home" is from the band's third album, before *Girls, Girls, Girls* and then *Dr. Feelgood*; they hadn't yet made it to the big cog.

Guns N' Roses wasn't really a hair metal band, but they were inextricable from the Sunset Strip scene. The "Welcome to the Jungle" video starts with Axl Rose as the pretty, naive ingenue stepping off the bus with his life packed in a suitcase. He's even chewing on a stalk of grass. This was the closest to the hair/glam look they really got—when he's onstage, Axl's hair is teased and sprayed and he's wearing visible eyeliner. The rest of the band just looks how they look. (The only thing that ever changes about Slash's look is whether he's holding a guitar or a bottle of Jack.) *Appetite for Destruction* put GNR at the big cog level, so when they released "Patience" as a single from their follow-up *G N' R Lies*, they were easily in a position to do an exhaustion porn video.

In my opinion, and also in the realm of undisputed fact, "Patience" is the greatest rock video of all time. I watch it at least once a week before bed. It's not a montage of live footage, more a short film that approximates a typical day in the life of a touring band. It was shot in LA's Ambassador Hotel, best known as the site of Bobby Kennedy's assassination.

Shots of the band playing the song are intercut with scenes of them hanging around the hotel: Duff McKagan is tall and sexy in a white blazer with no lapels, carrying a room-service tray. Slash reclines in bed, handling a large snake (literally) while a series of beautiful women in lingerie try to seduce him, dissolving into one another. They can't hold his attention; fame is boring. Steven Adler looks sheepish on a couch in the lobby, scratching his head with his drumsticks, while two women sitting next to him laugh and gossip and ignore him. Adler's there although the song is acoustic, with no drum part. (Dee Snider once said, of "unplugged" metal, "What's metal about that?!") It was his last video with the band, before they kicked him out for being too wasted to keep time. A writer I know, a fellow fan, once told me her favorite part of the video is when Adler stays occupied by playing with candles. My favorite part is when Axl watches the "Welcome to the Jungle" video in his hotel room, a visual echo of the parts in the "Welcome to the Jungle" video where Axl watches TV—in someone's apartment, through a store window on the street, strapped to a chair in a straitjacket. Screens within screens. In "Welcome to the Jungle," Axl can't look away (he's on some of the screens). In "Patience," he's slumped over with his chin in his hand: the banality of fame. He's sick of himself.

By the early nineties, people were tired of the nonstop party, the too-much-ness of hair metal. When Nikki Sixx got "the orgy of success, girls, and drugs" he had always wanted, he was "confronted with a new problem": "What do you do after the orgy?" What is left to desire? Everyone in Mötley Crüe eventually went to rehab. Hair metal was starting to look formulaic, plasticky. "It got so processed and so refined that it became pablum," Snider said. Grunge, with its apparent authenticity, its gestures toward a value system other than hedonism, was moving in to deliver the death blow. At the end of "When Metal Ruled the World," George Lynch from Dokken says he realized, "I gotta go buy a flannel shirt."

For me, "Patience" represents peak metal, the sliver of time when scene fatigue was setting in but it hadn't yet all gone to shit. Rock stars were still capable of magic. The video seems to know how ephemeral it is. The people in it keep fading to nothing—the staff, the groupies, the hotel guests. They go transparent and then disappear, like ghosts.

Same River, Same Man

I once admitted a fondness for *The Catcher in the Rye*, and somebody challenged me: "Read it again." I was kind of offended. It was true I hadn't read it in twenty-five years, but I read it twice in high school, at fifteen or sixteen, each time in the span of a day, and I remembered the feeling it gave me. This person was so confident I wouldn't like the book anymore, as an adult. I was confident I would—yet, I was reluctant to do it. I often reread dog-eared and underlined passages from books, and I reread whole poems, because I never seem to remember poems, even my favorite poems, when I'm not reading them. But I rarely reread whole books, nonfiction or fiction. It doesn't suit my constitution.

In his essay "First Steps Toward a History of Reading," Robert Darnton describes a theory of "intensive" versus "extensive" reading attributed to the historian Rolf Engelsing, who argued that people read "intensively" between the Middle Ages and the eighteenth century: "They had only a few books—the Bible, an almanac, a devotional work or two—and they read them over and over again, usually aloud and in groups, so that a narrow range of traditional literature became deeply impressed on their consciousness," Darnton writes. After that, supposedly, people started reading "extensively": "They read all kinds of material, especially periodicals and newspapers, and read it only once."

Engelsing, Darnton writes, "does not produce much evidence for this hypothesis." But the model maps nicely to my own reading life. As a child I read intensively, the same few books over and over. They weren't world-historical or holy texts, but standard-issue YA, Louis Sachar and Judy Blume; books I came upon randomly, at bookfairs and in the strip-mall secondhand bookstore my mother took me to, or in the back of Waldenbooks or B. Dalton. A few were hand-me-downs from my mother's own childhood (like *The Boxcar Children*). It was partly an issue of access—I couldn't drive to the library myself or just buy more books whenever I wanted. I also found it comforting. Those books, like a song on a jukebox, produced a reliable feeling. Abruptly, in college, I stopped rereading, maybe because I was surrounded by people who had read more than me.

Some people say rereading is the only reading, but sometimes I think first readings are the only rereading. This isn't total nonsense. First readings are when I pay the most attention, do the most doubling back. They're when I have the most capacity for shock and joy. When I reread I am always comparing my experience with my first impression, a constant distraction; I am tempted to skip and skim, to get along with it and verify my memories already, my belief that I already know what I think. You can reread ad infinitum, but you can only read something for the first time once.

There are other anxieties. I'm running out of time to read all the books I want to, of course; of course my one life is getting on half over, if I'm lucky. But more so—it feels like people who urge you to reread books so you can form a new opinion, to update or overwrite the old one, want you to betray your younger self, as if the new opinion is better—as if my new self is better. Maybe I'm not any better? I think some books are better encountered when you've read less, lived less, and know less. You can't wait to read everything until you're wiser, nor can you already have read everything once. At some point, you just have to read things. I want to defend my fifteen-year-old self from that friend who said, "Read it again." That self only knew what she knew. That self wasn't *wrong*.

The summer I moved back to New England, after living in Denver for ten years, after living in Boston for ten before that, I decided to reread some books. Specifically, I wanted to revisit books from my youth, my deep youth—books that I dimly remembered, so they would feel almost like first readings. John and I went to the Book Barn, and I found one of those mass-market paperback copies of *The Catcher in the Rye* with the brick-red cover for a dollar. The copyright page says, "69 printings through 1989." The one I read in the nineties was black type on white, with a rainbow of diagonal lines in the upper-left corner. I read it in my childhood bedroom in my parents' house in El Paso, Texas, where I spent the first two decades of my life, where in high school I made a collage on one wall using magazine cut-ups and Scotch tape. When I moved out, my parents took it down and repainted. This time, I read it in my mother-in-law's house in Norwich, Connecticut, the house John grew up in. His old room still looks like the nineties. The wallpaper matches the bedspread.

"If you really want to hear about it," *The Catcher in the Rye* begins, the first thing you'll probably want to know is where I was born, and what my lousy childhood was like, and how my parents were occupied and all before they had me, and all that David Copperfield kind of crap, but I don't feel like going into it, if you want to know the truth. In the first place, that stuff bores me, and in the second place, my parents would have about two hemorrhages apiece if I told anything pretty personal about them.

I started the novel with some trepidation (what if I *was* wrong?) but quickly relaxed into it. Like *Huckleberry Finn*, it's mostly a voicey monologue, even voicier than I remembered, full of emphatic italics ("They're *nice* and all—I'm not saying that") and direct address, breaking the fourth wall. When Holden tells us about his little sister, Phoebe, he says, "You'd like her." It's a little bit dated and heavy-handed—if I read it for the first time in my forties, I probably wouldn't like it as much as I did at fifteen. But how can I know? As Holden says, "How do you know what you're going to do till you *do* it?" I can't know, but I can see why I liked it—it's not about some big subject that I couldn't understand or didn't care about, like so many "good" books I encountered at the time. It's just about the experience of being young, or young but on the edge-end of youth, when you don't fit in with kids anymore or adults quite yet. The stuff that happens in the novel, over several days, is mostly random and low-stakes. Like *Huckleberry Finn*, it's picaresque, and very funny.

I have a sense that I found Holden purely likable on the first read, a sense that I was fully charmed. On this read

he seems more unreliable to me, and a bad judge of his
own character. It's not necessarily a permanent character
flaw. He's grieving—we learn on page 38 that his younger
brother, Allie, has died of leukemia ("You'd have liked
him")—and he's depressed; he can't see what bad shape he's
in. He's a liar, which he knows, but he's lying even when
he doesn't think he's lying. The dialogue comes from inside the monologue, so how much of it can we trust? We
get both halves of conversations through him. This book
is often about the difference between what we say and what
we think—Holden hates phonies, but when he talks to his
old teacher, on his way to drop out of school, he says one
thing and thinks another:

> "Life *is* a game, boy. Life *is* a game that one plays ac-
> cording to the rules."
> "Yes, sir. I know it is. I know it."
> Game, my ass. Some game. If you get on the side
> where all the hot-shots are, then it's a game, all right—
> I'll admit that. But if you get on the other side, where
> there aren't any hot-shots, then what's a game about it?
> Nothing. No game.

He's playing the game here, telling his teacher what he
wants to hear. When Holden meets a classmate's mother
on a train, he starts "shooting the old crap around a little bit." He tells the woman that her son is very popular,
yet shy and modest—her son Ernest, "doubtless the biggest
bastard that ever went to Pencey . . . He was always going down the corridor, after he'd had a shower, snapping
his soggy old wet towel at people's asses. That's exactly the

kind of guy he was." Ernest's mother agrees that he's sensitive. Holden thinks, "About as sensitive as a goddamn toilet seat." Holden pretends to be grown up—standing to his full height and showing off his premature gray so he can order drinks at a bar—but he likes kids more than adults. Kids are genuine, grown-ups are fake, and at the edge-end of youth, he hates what he's becoming. Can you like Holden, as an adult? I can, but it's different. I don't *admire* him. He's pathetic, in both senses—tragically pitiable and also kind of disgusting. He's a "sad, screwed-up type guy," like he says of Hamlet. (Recently, watching a production of *Hamlet*, always surprised by how much the play contains, always more than I remember or seems possible, I thought: Memory is impoverished compared with experience—a good argument for rereading. But experience is richer than assumption or projection—a good argument for reading something new. I was surprised by the very first line I read of Proust.)

A little more than halfway through the book, Holden walks around Central Park in the cold, looking for his sister. (How did I picture the park as a teenager, before I'd been to New York City? I suppose I knew how it looked from movies. *Manhattan*, Whit Stillman's *Metropolitan*, which made me feel—and this is how I put it to myself at the time, in these exact words—*like I don't exist*, like Manhattan was the center of the universe and I was off in a distant arm of the spiral galaxy.) He remembers going to the Museum of Natural History almost weekly as a grade school student. "I get very happy when I think about it. Even now." He remembers the nice smell inside the auditorium—"it always smelled like it was raining outside, even if it wasn't, and you were in the only nice, dry, cosy place in the world"—and the sticky hand of the little girl he was partnered with. "The best thing, though," Holden says, "in that museum was that everything always stayed right where it was." As many times as you went,

> that Eskimo would still be just finished catching those two fish, the birds would still be on their way south, the deers would still be drinking out of that water hole, with their pretty antlers and their pretty, skinny legs . . . Nobody'd be different. The only thing that would be different would be *you*. Not that you'd be so much older or anything. It wouldn't be that exactly. You'd just be different, that's all. You'd have an overcoat on this time. Or the kid that was your partner in line the last time had got scarlet fever and you'd have a new partner . . . Or you'd just passed by one of those puddles in the street with gasoline rainbows in them. I mean you'd be *dif*ferent in some way—I can't explain what I mean.

It's too perfect to say, that's like *me*, with this book. If I still like the book, I'm not fundamentally different, but I'm different enough to make a difference. Part of the difference is that I can articulate now what I understood then more instinctively—which doesn't make the later reading experience better. In fact I feel like Salinger was writing for the inarticulate kid—he was writing more for me then than me now. I'm glad I read it first then, and whenever a friend says they've never read it, I tend to tell them it's too late now. I don't know if that's true, because I don't have the experience of reading it late, not for the first time, but I believe it to be true. I think I was right, at fifteen, to like it for the reasons I did. I wasn't wrong.

In the park, Holden thinks about Phoebe getting older, changing—it upsets him. He wants to keep her innocent. Holden has learned early that life gets harder and worse. "Certain things they should stay the way they are. You ought to be able to stick them in one of those big glass cases and just leave them alone." In this blue mood he meets his old girlfriend Sally, a phony, for a play, and then they go ice skating at her insistence. She wants to rent one of those "darling little skating skirts." "That's why she was so hot to go," Holden says. "They gave Sally this little blue butt-twitcher of a dress to wear. She really did look damn good in it, though. I have to admit it." For some reason this is one of the scenes I most vividly remembered through the years, Sally showing off her cute ass, and Holden barely tolerating Sally, finally insulting her and making her cry. A few chapters later, he sneaks into his parents' apartment—they don't know he dropped out of school yet—to see Phoebe. I remembered this part too. Out of all the scenes in the book, the ones that stuck with me were the ice-skating scene, and sexy Stradlater telling Holden about his date with Jane, a girl Holden had loved, agitating him unto violence, and then visiting Phoebe in her pajamas, and then the scene in the stairwell at Phoebe's school, where Holden had also gone, with the "Fuck you" scrawled on the wall, which he tries to rub off. It's the encroachment of the dirty, dark world of adults, inside this world of children, that disgusts him. "It wouldn't come off. It's hopeless anyway. If you had a million years to do it in, you couldn't rub out even *half* the 'Fuck you' signs in the world. It's impossible."

All these scenes felt good to reread too, either funny or moving—intense moments of escape or transgression. I remembered these, and I forgot all the bad parts, the parts I guess that were supposed to jump out when I was told to "read it again." I'd forgotten the really homophobic and misogynist stuff. There's not a ton of it, but it's there and I'd forgotten. It's a gift when you can do that, when you can forget. I want to protect these good parts I remember, the parts I loved at fifteen and forty-two, to preserve them in their glass case. I think it's beautiful, still, that Holden wants to keep the schoolchildren innocent, that he wants to protect them, because *he* can't be protected anymore, he thinks. Like one of Rilke's angels, he wants to protect kids from pain, from learning what life is like with its "Fuck you" graffiti everywhere. He thinks it's too late for him, that he can't go home and can't go back to school. But he can still catch these kids—"if a body catch a body coming through the rye"—before they run off the cliff edge of youth.

John has a theory that everyone is either a squid or an eel. Baby squids are born as perfectly formed but teeny versions of their later selves. Eels go through radical changes over the course of one lifetime, to the degree that scientists used to think eels at different life stages were totally different types of eel. John claims he is an eel, and I am a squid. When we met, I'd sometimes ask him what he thought of one book or another, and he would say he didn't know—he had read it, but ten or fifteen years earlier, and no longer trusted his opinion. Every five to ten years, he feels like a different self. Over the many years he's known me, he says,

I've been strikingly consistent. I think about this theory whenever I revisit a book or a movie, half expecting my opinion to change, and find that I feel much the same: it's the same river and I am the same man. I appreciate *Hamlet* much more than I used to, but it's too long and some of it is boring. When I was bored during *Hamlet* as a kid, I wasn't wrong.

I've been rereading books in part to test my squidness. Reading *Catcher in the Rye* reinforced my squidness, but made me overconfident. Next I started *Breakfast of Champions* by Vonnegut, which I adored at sixteen. I only made it through one chapter. "Trout and Hoover were citizens of the United States of America, a country which was called America for short. This was their national anthem, which was pure balderdash, like so much they were expected to take seriously." It was too straightforward. I thought to myself, *This book was written for children.* Why didn't I think that of the Salinger? Or why did I think the same, but not in a negative way? In *The Child That Books Built*, Francis Spufford remarks that when reading *Catcher* as an adolescent, "usually you feel that he's doing being a lost boy more completely than you." You see the irony more as an adult—this is the artful double exposure of the book—but it works either way. Holden works as a character whether you envy or pity him. I sometimes think what makes a book a classic is that it's appealing to young people, yet belongs to a grown-up moral world. I think great books engender a feeling of longing, something just out of reach. When you're young, it's the grown-up world out of reach; when you're older, it's the freedom of youth. Each looks like freedom to the other.

I decided to try *Rabbit, Run*. As far as I recall, I read

it during my senior year of high school, and immediately felt it was my favorite book. I read the other Rabbit books in college, and a few more Updike novels in my twenties, but none of them struck me as much. Still, I have remained defensive of Updike—it seems like nobody likes him anymore, he's become a laughable figure, and I'm protective of his old corpse. We went back to the Book Barn and I found a used copy, the trade paperback with a photo of a basketball on the cover—so lazy. (I told a friend how much I hated the cover, and he protested that it works because it's about an aging athlete. "It's not about a *basketball*, David," I shouted, "it's about *lost youth*!") It was slow to get into, with meandering slow moody sentences, not written for children: "This farmhouse, which once commanded half of the acreage the town is now built on, still retains, behind a shattered and vandalized fence, its yard, a junkheap of brown stalks and eroded timber that will in the summer bloom with an unwanted wealth of weeds, waxy green wands and milky pods of silk seeds and airy yellow heads almost liquid with pollen." There's a smothering humidity to the prose. "Then, safe on the firm blacktop, you can decide whether to walk back down home or to hike up to the Pinnacle Hotel for a candy bar and a view of Brewer spread out like a carpet, a red city, where they paint wood, tin, even red bricks red, an orange rose flowerpot red that is unlike the color of any other city in the world yet to the children of the county is the only color of cities, the color all cities are." And then here and there, amid this thick damp description, a short clean sentence that's like coming up for air: "There was no sunshine in it."

About fifty pages in I was wondering, why did I love this

book about lost youth so much when I was young, before I'd lost anything? Did we know, a little bit, while still in youth, how precious it was? I was not very into the book, at that point. I couldn't remember what I'd liked about it at seventeen; it gave me an eellike feeling. On the page torn from a notepad I was using as a bookmark, I wrote: *I am disappointed in Updike. I wish it was funny, at all.* It was sometimes beautiful—I love that list of songs on the radio, the first time he runs away, that particular way of marking passed time—but never funny; somehow baggy, with too much fabric; and often so mean it's repulsive. It's Rabbit, Harry "Rabbit" Angstrom, that's mean and not the novel, I think; I don't think the novel is on Rabbit's side exactly. We are not permitted to stay too close to Harry and side with him too much. But still, it's hard to watch. That's how it feels, that you're *watching* him be mean to his poor wife, Janice. Janice loves him, but she knows he's vile. On page 80, he tells Ruth, the woman he's just met that he's about to shack up with, that he'll run out for groceries and she can make them lunch. "You said last night you liked to cook." "I said I used to." "Well, if you used to you still do." That's a squid thing to say! The feeling of starting to like a thing I used to hate is pleasurable, I've noticed, but not the reverse. It's a pleasurable kind of cheating, a bending of rules, as opposed to a betrayal of the whole system.

Around page 90, just when I thought I had seen enough and was about to stop reading, it suddenly got a little funny—as if wishes worked. Right around where Harry runs into Reverend Eccles, it suddenly got really good, the way the whole mood of a party can change when someone new walks in. I hadn't remembered the character of Eccles, who takes an interest in Harry, who wants to save Harry's marriage and be Harry's friend. I think Eccles saves the novel. When Eccles's wife asks him, "Why must you spend your life chasing after that worthless heel?" he responds, "He's not worthless. I love him." That's Updike, I realize now—I don't think I would have seen it back then. He loves Rabbit, the way God loves all his little sinners. It made me love him too—because I did love Rabbit at seventeen, as I'd loved Holden before him—this insistence that he deserves attention, that terrible people can still be tragic and worthy of love. There's a complexity to the morals, and a sophistication to the point of view, that I have trouble believing I would have grasped on first read. Eccles does succeed in convincing Harry to return to his wife when she goes into labor with their second child. He's so relieved to be forgiven, relieved that neither of them dies in childbirth, which would seem just punishment, that they spend a month or two in hazy bliss. The happiness here is a false bottom. He tries to seduce her one night before she's ready. She feels used and turns him away. Angry, he gets up to leave again. "Why can't you try to imagine how I *feel*? I've just had a baby," she says. "I can," he says, "I can but I don't want to, it's not the thing, the thing is how *I* feel." When Janice wonders of Harry, after he's gone, "What was so precious about him?" we understand it's that he's in a novel, because the novel's about him. Updike, the God of this novel, can imagine how Janice feels—he understands why Janice drinks, the same reason Rabbit runs, for freedom. (She is stuck, either stuck with Harry or stuck alone, but a drink helps a little, it makes "the edges nice and rainbowy.") He withholds that understanding, that ability or willingness, from

Harry, so Harry can act as he does, selfishly, cruelly. So we can live vicariously through Harry's escapes, and then see him punished for his mistakes.

I once read that we remember experiences by either their peak of intensity or what happens at the end—that people may forget the pain of childbirth, in the classic example, because it ends so happily. I wonder if that happened for me with *Rabbit, Run*. It was the tub scene I remembered most clearly, though I had a false memory of what she'd been drinking. (I thought it was Campari, but it's whiskey. The Campari I must have imported from a later novel, maybe *Rabbit Is Rich*.) She starts drinking and I saw it coming, as I couldn't have before, because I didn't know anything about the plot the first time I read it. This time, when Janice turns the faucet on, I physically shook my head—*don't do it*. The writing in this passage, too, is beautiful, so close we are to Janice, with Janice into morning as she tries to drink her fear away. "As she sits there watching the blank radiance a feeling of some other person standing behind her makes her snap her head several times. She is very quick about it but there is always a space she can't see, which the other person could dodge into if he's there." What is the presence, the ghost of Rabbit? Is it us? She keeps drinking, "just to keep sealed shut the great hole"—"she feels like a rainbow." And when she loses her grip on the baby in the tub, "it is only a moment, but a moment dragged out in a thicker time." The last line of this passage can almost make me cry, even read in isolation: "Her sense of the third person with them widens enormously, and she knows, knows, while knocks sound at the door, that the worst thing that has ever happened to any woman in the world has happened to her."

Eccles's wife says, "You never should have brought them back together"—implicating him. Eccles calls Harry and tells him, "A terrible thing has happened to us." That *us* is Eccles and Harry, Eccles and God and Harry—or author and character, author and reader. We're all in this mess together, we all murdered the baby. In the aftermath Harry seems to *almost* know, to finally know, he's been in the wrong—"He feels he will never resist anything again"—but he can't quite know it, because what held him back from going home was "the feeling that somewhere there was something better for him." Something better, that is, than settling down with the first woman he got pregnant, who is likewise forced to settle for him; something better than a job on his father-in-law's car lot, when he used to know the glory of the court. This is the complexity I mean, this teetering refusal to side quite for or against Harry Angstrom. The choice between freedom and duty is not an easy choice, the book allows, not actually. And it's not a question of fairness. That wanting more than life usually offers is somehow evil—this is a tragedy.

It's not at all like I remembered, I kept telling people, when I mentioned I was reading *Rabbit, Run*. But really, I remembered barely anything about it. Just a couple of scenes—that first time in the bar, drinking daiquiris, with his old coach and Ruth, and the bathtub—and the general idea of lost youth. And it's not lost innocence. Youth isn't innocence, it's possibility.

I don't really have a favorite book, but I sometimes think *Point Break* is my favorite movie. It depends what one means

by "favorite." Is it the same as your desert island movie? Do
I think it's the *best* movie? It depends what you mean when
you say something's *good*. There's a sense in which it's not a
good movie at all—I mean, of course, the 1991 *Point Break*,
starring Patrick Swayze and Keanu Reeves, which is in some
ways a ridiculous, even stupid movie—yet I am basically
always up for watching it, and right when it's over, I always
sort of want to watch it again.

I sometimes think there's a theoretical maximum to the
appreciable quality of art—a physical limit, like the speed
of light, to how much greatness I can experience. There
are many technically better movies than *Point Break*, many
movies with more historical significance. But I can only enjoy them as much as *Point Break*, because *Point Break* is the
limit for greatness. As the first review on Amazon puts it,
"If you don't like this movie, you don't like movies." In this
sense, it *is* the best movie. You can't go faster than the speed
of light.

I saw it for the first time in the early nineties, but not
in the theater. In my memory it was daytime, either a summer or a weekend afternoon, and my older brother and I
watched it on cable, not knowing anything about it, in-
creasingly riveted, giddy. We used to sit on the floor in the
den right in front of the TV, and we kept inching closer to
the screen, as the tension kept ratcheting up. It ratchets up
when FBI agent Angelo Pappas, played by Gary Busey, tells
his new partner Johnny Utah, played by Keanu, his theory on the case he's been working on for years: a group of
bank robbers known as the Ex-Presidents are surfers. (The
guy who came up with the idea for the movie—"Surfers
who rob banks. And an FBI agent that's a good athlete that

goes undercover among those surfers"—said it "wasn't that original an idea, there's only like ten ideas"!) It ratchets up when Johnny, a former star quarterback, buys a surfboard and nearly drowns trying to use it. He is dragged to shore by Tyler, played by Lori Petty. Johnny decides to use her to get in with the locals, digging up dirt on her past, finding out where she works. It ratchets up when he tells her his parents died in a car wreck, knowing hers both died in a plane crash, so she'll teach him how to surf. It's so interesting when actors have to lie or act in a role—it's like a frame narrative, acting in quotation marks. The movies suggest that FBI agents must have an interest in acting; they have to be willing to go undercover.

It ratchets up again the night of their first lesson, when Johnny meets Bodhi, played by Patrick Swayze, on the beach. Bodhi is short for "bodhisattva": "a person who is able to reach nirvana but delays doing so out of compassion in order to save suffering beings." Surfing movies are always about initiation. There's a fool who knows nothing—about surfing, the ocean, this connection between waves and nirvana. The sea as beyond. In *Point Break*, Johnny is a double initiate, doubly ignorant and dangerous. In one of the first scenes, his boss, Ben Harp, played by John C. McGinley, tells him, "You know nothing. In fact, you know less than nothing. If you even knew that you knew nothing, then that would be something, but you don't." Why is that? Why is there always a fool? In movies, surfing is knowledge, but also a manifestation of ego. The fool is a foil against the guru, the bodhisattva. Without the fool, the guru wouldn't know all; he'd know nothing also. They all play a game of football in the dark, lit by campfire and jeep headlights.

This is when it starts getting really good, when the split occurs, the fissure—Bodhi recognizes Johnny ("The Ohio State Buckeyes, all-conference!"), so they know something real about him. Not everything, of course. They don't know the pretty fool is a cop. Johnny sticks around to insinuate their world, but really falls in love with Tyler, and with surfing.

Johnny thinks he's found his guys when some territorial "Nazi assholes" try to beat him up on the beach—surfers are notoriously territorial, at least in the movies—but Bodhi shows up and the two of them beat up the assholes instead. Johnny sets up a raid on the guys' house, then goes night-surfing with Tyler ("At least nobody's going to see how bad you are," she says) and sleeps on the beach. He's late to his own raid, and things ratchet up again. A surfer played by Anthony Kiedis, of the Red Hot Chili Peppers, gets his foot shot to shreds. One of the assholes tries to push Johnny's face into a lawnmower; he's less than an inch from the blur of blades, his resistance giving out, when Pappas shoots out the motor and saves him. (This part was always hard to watch, but even more so now that I know the pain of going to work underslept.) It's all a mistake. They're into drugs but not bank robbery, and in the course of events Pappas and Johnny have to kill two or three of the assholes. "I hate that," Pappas says, "it looks bad on my report." This is the system the director Kathryn Bigelow refers to in a documentary about the making of *Point Break*. It's why she was attracted to the movie: "It's a system versus the anti-system." It's cops versus robbers—Robin Hood shit. It's Holden versus school, Rabbit versus church and society.

Johnny finally realizes Bodhi and his friends are the

bank robbers. He trails them for a day or so and figures out their plan. Johnny and Pappas stake out the scene of the next heist, but they almost miss the whole thing—the Ex-Presidents are known for getting in and out in ninety seconds, never shooting anybody, never going for the vault—while ordering sandwiches. (In that same documentary, Swayze remarks on Busey's "fabulously interesting choices," then quotes Busey's famous line: "Utah! Get me two!") Then follows a car chase, and then an awesome foot chase, Johnny chasing Bodhi through a residential neighborhood in LA, down alleys and through houses and backyards. It's Keanu but it wasn't actually Swayze; he was indisposed that day, and his character is in disguise anyway, wearing a suit and a rubber Ronald Reagan mask, the kind that pulls over your whole head. (A movie with this many masks and body doubles asks a lot of trust from its audience. The first time we watch Bodhi surf, it's clearly not Patrick Swayze. It makes me think of a poster for the animated movie *Polar Express*, dubbed into German, that a friend once saw in Berlin—in what sense was it "starring Tom Hanks"?) Johnny isn't masked, so the act is now threatened, the fracture, but not entirely dissolved—Bodhi knows Johnny's a cop, but he doesn't know if Johnny knows he, the Ex-President, is Bodhi. They sort of make eye contact, from maybe fifty yards away—it's a little hard to tell, in movie space. Johnny's knee is blown out, but he has Bodhi in his sights and he's a crack shot (Pappas: "When you shoot, you don't miss"). Bodhi holds still, almost daring him to shoot. Ratchet up, ratchet up. I always feel I have to move during this scene, to lean forward, move my legs, get closer to the screen. Johnny can't do it; he kind of loves

Bodhi. His friend, his enemy—as Guy asks of Bruno, when Bruno falls overboard, in *Strangers on a Train*, "Where was his friend, his brother?" Johnny unloads his magazine into the air and screams.

At this point Bodhi starts to lose the thread. He starts talking about "stakes" and "the game." Young Grommet, the one who wears the LBJ mask, played by a surfer named BoJesse Christopher, says, "Fuck the stakes, Bodhi! I mean the only person this is a game to is you! This is real! I mean this is serious shit and I, for one, am scared." Then they all show up at Johnny's, to take him someplace, but friendly: "You are going to *love this*." Johnny's knee and his face are all fucked up. Temporarily, that undissolved, unresolved split becomes strange. It's hard to track who knows what. Why are they pretending? Which quotes are we in?

The first skydiving scene is somewhat a release from the tension, the high torque. (*Point Break* always seems to contain another scene, another act, to hold more than you remember, like *Hamlet*. I can't believe it's only two hours long.) The music in this scene is soaring, uplifting—"the orchestral tones are at times euphoric," as one review of the score put it. Their movements are balletic. "Sex with the gods!" one of them cries. All the dialogue in these scenes took "poetic license," in Swayze's language—you can't actually talk, or hear, I guess, when you're free-falling in high winds. Swayze really did dive out of planes, so many times in fact that the crew finally asked him to stop for insurance reasons, but for the close-ups, the stunt coordinator rigged up a circle of cranes to hover the actors, who were filmed with a floating camera. Bigelow must not have been quite as obsessed with authenticity as her then-husband James

Cameron, who insisted on filming all the diving scenes in *The Abyss* "wet for wet"—meaning, if the characters were supposed to be underwater, the actors had to be underwater as well—almost killing Ed Harris in the process. Now that Bodhi has lost it, he's breaking his own rules. When they rob the last bank they go for the vault. A big guy on the floor softly whispers to a nearby security guard: *I'm a cop.* He gestures toward his concealed weapon. By this time, it's an anti-cop movie. The security guard cringes and we cringe with him, he cringes for us. No, we think, no—*don't do it!* The cop doesn't help anything. A bunch of people get shot, he gets shot himself.

I wonder how much poetic license was involved in the second skydiving scene, when Johnny jumps out of the plane without a chute, holding nothing but a handgun. Obviously, this is insane, but what I mean is, is it physically possible that he could catch up with Bodhi, who had jumped out fifteen seconds earlier, and was that much closer to the earth? It's a pointless question, like asking if Keanu is a good actor. I remember how shocked we were the first time we watched it, when he jumps. My brother has a particular, high-pitched laugh that only comes out when he's really surprised, and he laughed like that then, and I can hear it now. It's like the wrench has been twisted so tight something breaks. Euphoria. Insanity.

When I stopped rereading books, I didn't stop rewatching movies. It doesn't take as much time, for one thing. And movies I've watched many times are a very great comfort to me. It's what I do when I'm too sick, exhausted, or anxious to read. I sometimes replay movies in my head to relax when I can't fall asleep. Outside of my squidness, there remains a question: Would I get bored of *Point Break* or *Moby-Dick* on a desert island? A Twitter acquaintance told me he once spent a summer in a beach house on the Jersey shore with "no TV hookup and one single tape for the VCR: *Point Break*." He watched it over and over, "like it was the only thing ever filmed . . . it was glorious." Is good art exhaustible? To quote Johnny Utah, when Ben Harp wonders if the FBI has "an asshole shortage": "Not so far."

Rewatching *Point Break*, in order to take notes and write about it, wasn't quite the sublime experience of watching it to watch it. So after writing about it, I watched it again, the following night. This didn't feel very different from watching it again after one or two years. This is part of the difference between books and movies. Books take so much more time to invest in, to get interesting again, that they give me time to change. I must be changing all the time, but day to day, or year to year, the intervals are too small to notice. I'm not the same man, but I almost am. Squids may not become unrecognizable with age, but they get larger and more complicated. You can tell their age by "growth rings," as with trees. And every time I watch *Point Break*, I contain more complication. I still contain a child and a fool inside me; I have all their memories. I know more, but I still know nothing.

Selected Bibliography

Alexander, Christopher, Sara Ishikawa, and Murray Silverstein, with Max Jacobson, Ingrid Fiksdahl-King, and Shlomo Angel. *A Pattern Language: Towns, Buildings, Construction*. New York: Oxford University Press, 1977.

Bachelard, Gaston. *The Poetics of Space*. Translated by Maria Jolas. Boston: Beacon Press, 1994.

Baudelaire, Charles. *Les Fleurs du mal*. Paris: Poulet-Malassis & De Broise, 1857.

———. *The Painter of Modern Life and Other Essays*. Translated by Jonathan Mayne. New York: Phaidon, 1995.

Becker, Ernest. *The Denial of Death*. New York: Free Press, 1973.

Berryman, John. *The Dream Songs*. New York: Farrar, Straus and Giroux, 2014.

Birkerts, Sven. *The Gutenberg Elegies: The Fate of Reading in an Electronic Age*. New York: Faber and Faber, 2006.

Borges, Jorge Luis. *Labyrinths*. Edited by Donald A. Yates and James E. Irby. New York: New Directions, 1962.

Bradbury, Ray. *Fahrenheit 451*. New York: Del Rey, 1987.

Bryson, Bill. *At Home: A Short History of Private Life*. New York: Doubleday, 2010.

Cacioppo, John T., and William Patrick. *Loneliness: Human Nature and the Need for Social Connection*. New York: W. W. Norton and Company, 2009.

Capote, Truman. *Breakfast at Tiffany's*. New York: Random House, 1958.

Carrington, Leonora. *Down Below*. New York: NYRB Classics, 2017.

———. *The Hearing Trumpet*. New York: NYRB Classics, 2021.

Castro, Jordan. *The Novelist*. New York: Soft Skull, 2022.

Clark, Heather. *Red Comet: The Short Life and Blazing Art of Sylvia Plath*. New York: Knopf, 2020.

Collins, Phil. *Not Dead Yet: The Memoir*. New York: Crown Archetype, 2016.

Contemporary American Poetry, Sixth Edition. Edited by A. Poulin, Jr. Boston: Houghton Mifflin Company, 1996.

Cotter, John. *Under the Small Lights*. Oxford, OH: Miami University Press, 2010.

Czapski, Józef. *Lost Time: Lectures on Proust in a Soviet Prison Camp*. Translated by Eric Karpeles. New York: NYRB Classics, 2018.

D'Arcy, Barbara. *Bloomingdale's Book of Home Decorating*. New York: Harper and Row, 1973.

Darnton, Robert. *The Kiss of Lamourette: Reflections in Cultural History*. New York: W. W. Norton and Company, 1990.

De Botton, Alain. *The Architecture of Happiness*. New York: Vintage, 2008.

Didion, Joan. *Let Me Tell You What I Mean*. New York: Knopf, 2021.

Dillon, Brian. *Suppose a Sentence*. New York: New York Review Books, 2020.

Eliot, T. S. *The Waste Land, and Other Poems*. New York: Harvest Books, 1988.

Fisher, Mark. *The Weird and the Eerie*. New York: Repeater, 2017.

Fitzgerald, F. Scott. *The Great Gatsby*. New York: Scribner, 1996.

Flaubert, Gustave. *Madame Bovary*. Translated by Lydia Davis. New York: Penguin, 2010.

Gaddis, William. *The Recognitions*. New York: Harcourt, Brace, 1955.

Ginzburg, Natalia. *Family Lexicon*. Translated by Jenny McPhee. New York: NYRB Classics, 2017.

Hardwick, Elizabeth. *Seduction and Betrayal: Women and Literature*. New York: Random House, 1974.

Hemingway, Ernest. *A Moveable Feast*. New York: Bantam, 1970.

Henkin, David M. *The Week: A History of the Unnatural Rhythms That Made Us Who We Are*. New Haven, CT: Yale University Press, 2021.

Highsmith, Patricia. *Strangers on a Train*. New York: W. W. Norton and Company, 2001.

Hughes, Richard. *A High Wind in Jamaica*. New York: NYRB Classics, 1999.

Jacobson, Mark. "For the Money." In *Why I Write: Thoughts on the*

Craft of Fiction, edited by Will Blythe, 116–23. Boston: Back Bay Books, 1999.

Kafka, Franz. *The Diaries of Franz Kafka, 1910–1923*. Edited by Max Brod. New York: Schocken, 1988.

Knausgård, Linda Boström. *Welcome to America*. Translated by Martin Aiken. New York: World Editions, 2019.

Lee, Tommy, Vince Neil, Mick Mars, and Nikki Sixx, with Neil Strauss. *The Dirt: Confessions of the World's Most Notorious Rock Band*. New York: Dey Street Books, 2002.

Lerner, Ben. *10:04*. New York: Farrar, Straus and Giroux, 2014.

Malcolm, Janet. *The Silent Woman: Sylvia Plath and Ted Hughes*. New York: Vintage, 1993.

Manguso, Sarah. *Ongoingness: The End of a Diary*. Minneapolis, MN: Graywolf, 2015.

Marías, Javier. *Between Eternities and Other Writings*. Translated by Margaret Jull Costa. New York: Vintage, 2018.

———. *The Infatuations*. Translated by Margaret Jull Costa. New York: Vintage, 2014.

McCullers, Carson. *The Member of the Wedding*. New York: Bantam, 1981.

Mellor, Anne K. *Mary Shelley: Her Life, Her Fiction, Her Monsters*. New York: Routledge, 1989.

Moschovakis, Anna. *Eleanor, or, The Rejection of the Progress of Love*. Minneapolis, MN: Coffee House, 2018.

O'Hara, John. *Appointment in Samarra*. New York: Vintage, 1982.

The Paris Review Interviews, Volume II. Edited by Philip Gourevitch. New York: Picador, 2007.

The Paris Review Interviews, Volume III. Edited by Philip Gourevitch. New York: Picador, 2008.

Patchett, Ann. "Writing and a Life Lived Well: Notes on Allan Gurganus." In *Why I Write: Thoughts on the Craft of Fiction*, edited by Will Blythe, 61–68. Boston: Back Bay Books, 1999.

Plath, Sylvia. *The Bell Jar*. New York: Harper Perennial, 2005.

———. *The Collected Poems*. Edited by Ted Hughes. New York: Harper Perennial, 1992.

———. *Mary Ventura and the Ninth Kingdom: A Story*. New York: Harper, 2019.

———. *The Unabridged Journals of Sylvia Plath*. Edited by Karen V. Kukil. New York: Anchor, 2000.

Podhoretz, Norman. *Making It*. New York: NYRB Classics, 2017.

Postman, Neil. *The Disappearance of Childhood.* New York: Vintage, 1994.

Price, Jill, with Bart Davis. *The Woman Who Can't Forget.* New York: Free Press, 2008.

Proust, Marcel. *Swann's Way.* Translated by C. K. Scott Moncrieff and Terence Kilmartin. New York: Vintage, 1989.

Ray, Rachael. *My Year in Meals.* New York: Atria, 2012.

Rilke, Rainer Maria. *The Dark Interval: Letters on Loss, Grief, and Transformation.* Translated by Ulrich Baer. New York: Modern Library, 2018.

———. *The Notebooks of Malte Laurids Brigge.* Translated by Stephen Mitchell. New York: Vintage, 1982.

———. *The Selected Poetry of Rainer Maria Rilke.* Translated by Stephen Mitchell. New York: Vintage, 1982.

Salinger, J. D. *The Catcher in the Rye.* New York: Bantam, 1964.

Salter, James. "Some for Glory, Some for Praise." In *Why I Write: Thoughts on the Craft of Fiction,* edited by Will Blythe, 34–40. Boston: Back Bay Books, 1999.

Shelley, Mary. *Frankenstein.* New York: Palgrave Macmillan, 2000.

Sontag, Susan. *Reborn: Journals & Notebooks, 1947–1963.* Edited by David Rieff. New York: Picador, 2009.

Spufford, Francis. *The Child That Books Built: A Memoir of Childhood and Reading.* London: Faber and Faber, 2002.

Steele, Richard. "Twenty-Four Hours in London." In *The Art of the Personal Essay: An Anthology from the Classical Era to the Present,* edited by Phillip Lopate, 129–32. New York: Anchor, 1995.

Stevenson, Robert Louis. *Dr. Jekyll and Mr. Hyde.* New York: Bantam, 1981.

Strout, Elizabeth. *My Name Is Lucy Barton.* New York: Random House, 2016.

Styron, William. *Darkness Visible: A Memoir of Madness.* New York: Vintage, 1992.

Tanizaki, Junichiro. "In Praise of Shadows." In *The Art of the Personal Essay: An Anthology from the Classical Era to the Present,* edited by Phillip Lopate, 335–62. New York: Anchor, 1995.

Updike, John. *Rabbit, Run.* New York: Fawcett Books, 1996.

Venturi, Robert. *Complexity and Contradiction in Architecture.* New York: The Museum of Modern Art, 1977.

Vidal, Gore. *Palimpsest.* New York: Random House, 1995.

Vollman, William. "Writing." In *Why I Write: Thoughts on the Craft of Fiction*, edited by Will Blythe, 110–15. Boston: Back Bay Books, 1999.

Von Kleist, Heinrich. *Michael Kohlhaas*. Translated by Michael Hofmann. New York: New Directions, 2020.

Vonnegut, Kurt. *Breakfast of Champions*. New York: Delacorte Press, 1973.

Wallace, David Foster. "The Nature of the Fun." In *Why I Write: Thoughts on the Craft of Fiction*, edited by Will Blythe, 140–45. Boston: Back Bay Books, 1999.

Waugh, Evelyn. *A Handful of Dust*. London: Penguin, 2003.

Wharton, Edith. *The House of Mirth*. New York: Scribner, 1995.

Williams, Joy. "Uncanny the Singing That Comes from Certain Husks." In *Why I Write: Thoughts on the Craft of Fiction*, edited by Will Blythe, 5–12. Boston: Back Bay Books, 1999.

Woolf, Virginia. "Street Haunting." In *The Art of the Personal Essay: An Anthology from the Classical Era to the Present*, edited by Phillip Lopate, 256–64. New York: Anchor, 1995.

———. *A Writer's Diary: Being Extracts from the Diary of Virginia Woolf*. Edited by Leonard Woolf. New York: Mariner, 2003.

Acknowledgments

Some of these essays, sometimes in part or in earlier versions, were originally published in the following publications: *Harper's Magazine*, *The New York Review of Books*, *The New York Times Magazine*, *The Paris Review Daily*, *Poetry Foundation*, and *The Yale Review*. Thank you to the editors I worked with on these pieces: Nitsuh Abebe, Sophie Haigney, Jeremy Lybarger, Meghan O'Rourke, Jana Prikryl, Matthew Sherrill, Nadja Spiegelman, and Emily Stokes. Parts of "Nostalgia for a Less Innocent Time" appeared in the March Badness tournament in 2020; thank you to Ander Monson.

Thank you to my agent, Monika Woods, and my editor, Milo Walls, and the rest of the team at FSG. Special thanks to Mitzi Angel, Jenna Johnson, and Julia Ringo.

For kindness, friendship, advice, or support of other and various kinds during the writing of this book, thank you to Matt Bell, Sommer Browning, Isaac Butler, Kate Colby, Erin Costello, Jordan Ellenberg, V. V. Ganeshananthan, Alyssa Harad, Adalena Kavanagh, J. Robert Lennon, Elizabeth Mc-Cracken, Catherine Nichols, Jen Olsen, Kathleen Rooney, and Mike Walsh. Thank you to C in particular for reading so much of this book as it was written, and for all your listening. Thank you to my Denver family, in particular Kevin and Katie Caron and Kirsten Lewis. Thank you to my group chats, a daily source of joy and commiseration. Thank you to Linda Cotter for your love, generosity, and patience during 2022 in particular. Thank you to Erin Cotter for allowing me to finish this book in your former room. Thank you to my parents, Michael and Ann Gabbert, for endless support; I love you! Thank you to John Cotter for everything. I couldn't do this without you.